'None of us are immune from life's challenges. At some point in life – or for most of us, at many points in life – we are faced with immense struggles. The good thing is that now we have a road map on how to get through those struggles thanks to this book The Power of Little Steps. This beautiful guide is humbled by Sheila's personal anecdotes of her own struggles, allowing us to connect with her. It's like we are all on this journey together. Thank you, Sheila, for this important and wise body of work!'

TOM CRONIN, COACH, MEDITATION TEACHER AND PRODUCER OF THE PORTAL (FILM AND BOOK)

'I always believed that by 45, I'd have life all figured out. Yet, one of the most profound lessons we learn as we age is that life is a continuous, winding journey with unexpected turns. Sheila's The Power of Little Steps beautifully acknowledges this reality, offering both comfort and clarity. This book empowers you to embrace the moments when change is essential, providing practical tools to take those crucial steps toward a more authentic and fulfilling path. A must-read for anyone seeking genuine transformation.'

KATH HALING, COMPOSER, LYRICIST, PLAYWRIGHT

'The Power of Little Steps is a transformative guide that speaks directly to the heart of anyone feeling lost or overwhelmed by life's challenges. Sheila Vijeyarasa masterfully combines wisdom with actionable advice, empowering you to make meaningful changes, one small step at a time. This book is a beacon of hope for those ready to embrace their true path with courage and authenticity. A truly inspiring read that will stay with you long after the final page.'

NINA CONCEPCION, AUTHOR OF THE NAKED YOU: A GUIDE TO EMBRACING YOUR IMPERFECTIONS IN LIFE AND BUSINESS

'The Power of Little Steps is the ultimate guide for taking little brave acts every day and inching towards our dreams even if it is via our Plan B or C. Sheila captures the emotional struggles many of us face, with such intense understanding that it seems like she's a soul sister. This book embraces all levels of understanding from the grounded physical, the unseen emotional, right through to our spiritual connection with ourselves and the universe to break free of the struggles and come out the other side. Brave truths, brave questions and brave mantras are the ultimate recipe for self-responsibility and moving forward when stuck.'

ANNE MILES, FOUNDER OF SUITS&SNEAKERS MULTI AWARD–WINNING CONSCIOUS ENTREPRENEUR

'Sheila's writing is a beacon of wisdom, honesty and inspiration. Her latest book is a candid guide to navigating life's unpredictability, disappointments and change. She shares her own struggles, particularly with IVF, with a raw vulnerability that holds nothing back. This book speaks directly to our most challenging moments, urging us to embrace Plan C as the path we were always meant to follow. Sheila invites us to make space for healing, adopt a brave mindset and rediscover our future selves. Her words offer comfort and inspiration, reminding us that nothing is lost, nothing is wasted and it's never too late. A must-read for anyone facing tough times, this book overflows with hope, optimism and a bright vision for our future selves.'

JESSICA LEE, FOUNDER OF THE SPARK EFFECT, WELL-BEING WRITER, SPEAKER, COACH

'The Power of Little Steps is a profoundly inspirational guide that invites women to embark on a journey toward their wildest dreams. Sheila's raw honesty and deeply personal stories create a roadmap to self-discovery and empowerment, showing us the strength found in vulnerability and honest self-enquiry. This book equips readers with the tools to navigate life's challenges, tap into inner strength, and rise above obstacles with courage and resilience. A must-read for anyone seeking to live authentically and fulfil their dreams, it reminds us that even the smallest steps can lead to incredible transformation.'

NICKY PULLEN, FOUNDER OF TOGETHER WE RISE

'Sheila's warmth and wisdom come oozing through each page of this book. You can feel the care Sheila has taken to ensure the words hit straight from her heart to yours.'

ALISON DADDO, AUTHOR OF QUEEN MENOPAUSE: FINDING YOUR MAJESTY IN THE MAYHEM

'No matter whether it's on a stage, one-on-one or through words in a book, Sheila always manages to bring inspired energy into the room. The Power of Little Steps is by no means a small feat and its messages of hope, wisdom and courage will continue to resonate with readers for years to come. I feel blessed to have Sheila as a friend and am honoured to see her continue to smash glass ceilings time and time again.'

ANDRÉS ENGRACIA, AUTHOR OF PURE MAGIC ORACLE, DIVINE DOORS AND DRUID WISDOM

'A lived example of blooming later in life, Sheila shows how taking Plan C can be your homecoming. Even if you aren't where you want to be and things feel scattered, this book shares ways to find your happily ever after.'

TAMMI KIRKNESS, AUTHOR OF THE PANIC BUTTON BOOK AND WHY DO I FEEL SO WORRIED?

Create the life of your wildest dreams

The Power of Little Steps

by the author of *Brave*

Sheila Vijeyarasa

ROCKPOOL

Note: For privacy, some names have been changed in this book.

A Rockpool book
PO Box 252
Summer Hill
NSW 2130
Australia

rockpoolpublishing.com
Follow us! f ⓘ rockpoolpublishing
Tag your images with #rockpoolpublishing

ISBN: 9781922786180

Published in 2025 by Rockpool Publishing
Copyright text © Sheila Vijeyarasa 2025
Copyright design © Rockpool Publishing 2025

Design and typesetting by Sara Lindberg, Rockpool Publishing
Structural edit by Gabiann Marin
Copyedited by Heather Millar

A catalogue record for this
book is available from the
National Library of Australia

Printed and bound in China

10 9 8 7 6 5 4 3 2 1

For my beloved Tyson,
may we continue to create a life
of big miracles together.

A'ho

Contents

The power of little steps

'A woman makes a plan.'

– MAYE MUSK

Here I am, awkwardly squatting over the toilet, desperately trying to aim for this pregnancy test. But honestly, does it even matter if I make a mess right now? I'm in my mid-40s, and all I want, more than anything, is to be pregnant. My husband paces anxiously in the bedroom, his anticipation is palpable.

I finish up, still perched on the toilet, and glance to my right. I'm being watched. It's not just Tyson and me in our apartment today. A big production house camera stares back at me, red light blinking. My pregnancy test is being filmed.

This isn't just any pregnancy test – we're in the early stages of a documentary about our IVF journey for a major TV network in Australia. And as I sit here, with a camera capturing every awkward angle, I can't help but wonder: how did I get here? This wasn't the plan!

But life rarely unfolds according to anyone's carefully crafted initial plan, and when that plan fails — let's call it Plan A — it can leave us feeling as bewildered as I was that day. Sometimes just the faintest suggestion that life is veering off the path we anticipated can leave us completely stunned. We feel betrayed, like utter failures, and it's infuriating. We're left standing in the rubble of our expectations, wondering what the hell just happened.

Take a traditional Plan A: to get married in your 20s, have kids before your mid-30s, and retire with your partner in your 60s. That was my expectation. Sound familiar? But life looked at my plan, rolled its eyes, and said, 'Expecting to get married in your 20s? How about a series of awkward first dates instead?'

Let's get real. When does life ever go according to plan? It's like trying to follow a recipe, and halfway through you realise you're missing some of the key ingredients. The issue with any Plan A is that it might not be the right plan for you at all. And once you've etched it in stone, anything that strays from it feels like a disappointment. This is why we often see our replacement plan — Plan B — as a second-rate compromise compared to our shiny, original Plan A.

Just as many Plan As are bound to fail, so will many Plan Bs. Why? Because it's the same over-caffeinated, anxiety-ridden mindset that created both plans, with the same problems, fears, hesitations and uncertainties behind it. We often come up with our Plan Bs in a crisis or out of necessity, and rarely want to stray too far from our original plan. When we cling to Plan B like it's the last lifeboat on the *Titanic* — any deviation feels like a disaster. But when Plan B fails too, it can leave us feeling totally bereft. It's like we're stuck in a loop, trying to fix things with the same thinking that created the mess in the first place.

So, how do we navigate our way when we keep failing, detouring and stumbling? How do we deal with the emotional rollercoaster of the initial path of Plan A and the compromised path of Plan B and somehow find that elusive plan – our Plan C – that we can't see coming, but that brings us everything we ever wanted?

In my years of coaching, here's what I've figured out: Plan C isn't just another fallback plan; it's often the path that's most aligned with our true purpose and where we find real fulfilment. Plan C is where the magic happens, where big miracles transpire, where we discover what genuinely matters to us. It's what I like to call the unexpected path.

When carefully laid plans fail, it feels like the end of the world. But guess what? It's not. It's the beginning of something more meaningful. There's a strange kind of gratitude that kicks in when we see those failures for what they really are: stepping stones to something greater. It's like when you realise losing that job you thought you couldn't live without opened the door to starting your own business – one that fills you with more joy and purpose than you ever imagined.

Life's curveballs often force us into dramatic changes that we initially resist, yet those changes usually lead to a life better than we ever imagined. I've seen people go through gut-wrenching break-ups only to find their true love later in life. I've seen others lose everything they thought they wanted and gain something they never knew they needed.

And here's the beautiful part: we grow to like who we are because of these failures. We learn to embrace our scars and see them as badges of honour. They remind us of the battles we've fought and the strength we've found within ourselves. It's in those moments of struggle and reinvention that we become more resilient, more compassionate, more ourselves.

What if we let go of the idea that living the life of our wildest dreams involves sticking rigidly to a script? What if, instead, we mastered the art of amplifying our intuition during transitions, pivoting our plans with an unstoppable force, and cozying up to resilience as if it was our closest confidant? What if, instead of being disappointed when Plan A fails, we accepted that it is only an initial path *and* that Plan B, the compromised path, may fail too? We can then prepare ourselves to take the little steps needed to move forward towards a more innovative, unexpected path of Plan C – a plan that will lead to far more joy than we ever imagined.

Whether you're diving into motherhood, battling through IVF fertility treatments, making significant career leaps, dealing with an empty nest, enduring menopause, rocking single parenting, jumping back into the dating scene over 40, launching a side hustle, or reinventing yourself after a divorce, failure is part of the journey. And not just once, but often over and over again. Embrace the chaos, the failure, the unexpected turns. That's where life gets interesting.

We can face these failures more productively – and dare I say, bravely – through taking little steps towards our goals which lead to undertaking what I call *Little Brave Acts*. These acts are a way of saying, 'Yes, this is hard. Yes, I'm scared. But I'm still showing up.'

Little Brave Acts are those small, gutsy moves that keep us going, even when life feels like a hot mess. They remind us that we're tougher than we think, that we can handle the rollercoaster ride, and that every small step forward is a win. Every seemingly insignificant moment of bravery can pave the way for greatness. That's how we change our world – one little step at a time.

What I'm proposing is a dance with change. And yes, that one word is a source of much trepidation for most of us, consciously or subconsciously. Still, we all need to embrace change. Change is not just inevitable; it's the fertile ground from which personal growth blossoms, and the pathway to achieving the goals that will set your soul on fire.

This book serves as a clear roadmap to guide you through this dance with change, through life's various challenges, crises and upheavals.

How to work with this book

Whether you are familiar with concepts to do with healing, transformation and finding your purpose, or you are just starting out on your healing path and seeking a clear process of transformation to follow, this book is for you. Be prepared to dive deep, reflect with raw honesty and commit to navigating transitions with clear-eyed, solid intention.

Each part is a crucial step on your journey to a more authentic life. The first part delves into bravery – facing our fears and embracing a brave mindset. The second teaches the art of letting go – embracing failure, shedding guilt and shame, cocooning to heal and releasing outdated beliefs. The third part provides tools for transformation – self-love, setting boundaries, abandoning timelines and dreaming big. In the final section, we embrace pivoting, overcome imposter syndrome and cultivate the grit, resilience and rebellious thinking needed to open yourself up to a life of miracles – the life that's been waiting for you!

This book offers tools to assist you in the crucial work of mindset development, emotional mastery and spiritual growth. At the end of every chapter, you will discover a toolkit with the following:

Brave truths

These truths act as beacons, guiding you beyond your current status quo. Your inner compass will resonate with these points, signalling them as crucial to follow.

Brave questions

These questions prompt honest introspection. Don't underestimate the value of answering them, as there's wisdom within you waiting to unfold on the pages of your journal. When you answer these questions honestly, you will feel empowered to commit to your *Little Brave Acts*.

Brave mantras

Mantras or affirmations can bring focus and calm to your mind. The potency of your thoughts correlates with the power of your life. These phrases aid in reshaping your thinking and mindset. Your presence here is proof that you've heeded your inner guidance, ready to reclaim the courageous part of yourself that may have been adrift.

I honour your commitment to this brave work and eagerly anticipate being a companion as you take your first and continued little steps along your journey towards becoming the bravest version of yourself!

What powerful small steps will you make today?

Let the adventure begin . . .

With love,

Sheila V

PART 1
Being brave

CHAPTER 1

The brave mindset

*'Courage doesn't always roar. Sometimes courage
is the little voice at the end of the day
that says I'll try again tomorrow.'*

– MARY ANNE RADMACHER

Life throws all sorts of changes our way, demanding we embrace them. Some changes creep up on us, like the slow, painful realisation that the career you've poured your heart into isn't fulfilling you. Some hit like a freight train, such as finding out your IVF round has failed. Some come with the natural ebb and flow of life, like transitioning into an empty nest when your kids leave home. Others are catastrophic, like losing your house in a flood. Or maybe it's the unexpected end of a long-term relationship, or the shock of a health diagnosis that flips your world upside down.

Regardless of the specific transition you're facing, a new life will only take shape through the cumulative effect of small, consistent acts of bravery carried out daily and weekly. These *Little Brave Acts* will enable a journey of resilience and growth, anchored in the courage to face life's inevitable challenges.

First, let's get on the same page about bravery, because Hollywood's got it all wrong. According to the filmmakers, it's all about saving the world and doing crazy superhero stuff – flying through the air, defying the laws of physics, basically doing the impossible.

Then there's the rest of us, getting a thrill from something as simple as nailing a parallel park.

Here's the thing: real-life bravery isn't about being bulletproof or leaping off tall buildings in a single bound. It's more mundane and yet, a lot more relevant. Think about the quiet guts it takes to speak up in a meeting, or the vulnerability to say 'I love you' first. *This* is the kind of bravery that changed my life – and my clients' lives. It appears in small, quiet, often unassuming moments, too low key to celebrate on social media! That's why I call them *Little Brave Acts*.

Little Brave Acts may seem small, but they are not always easy. While we are taught from a very young age that bravery is a desirable quality, we may well have had parents or teachers who struggled to be brave themselves, or didn't allow us to be brave, often because the risk of failing or straying too far from the norm was high.

Without openly talking about bravery, without *real-life* bravery role-modelled for us consistently, bravery becomes a skill we have to painstakingly acquire as adults, and learning to be brave isn't exactly a walk in the park. There is no instruction manual to guide us through.

Perhaps the very first act of bravery is realising that the world around us – society, culture, even our own families – has fallen short in demonstrating and permitting us to embody true bravery.

The root of being truly brave lies in overcoming the fear of what others will think of us, learning to trust our intuition and inner resources, and acting immediately against the fear that rises within us. So, the first crucial step in embracing bravery is recognising that it is both an emotion *and* an action.

The bridge to empowerment

*'Courage is the most important of all the virtues,
because without courage you can't practice any other
virtue consistently. You can practice any virtue erratically,
but nothing consistently without courage.'*

– MAYA ANGELOU

Why is bravery an important emotion? Dr David Hawkins, a pioneer in the realm of human consciousness, embarked on a remarkable journey in the 1980s – to analyse and quantify human emotions. Imagine doing this at a time when the scientific community wasn't exactly cheering for notions like energy fields and how our emotions might significantly influence them.

At the core of Hawkins' research was an exploration of emotions and their impact on our consciousness – our state of mind. He introduced a calibrated scale ranging from 0 to 1,000, where higher levels on the scale represented positive emotions such as love, joy and peace. Conversely, lower levels on the scale encompassed negative emotions such as fear, anger and guilt. Dr Hawkins discovered that when you're riding high on positive emotions, your vitality and energy soar. And when you're stuck in the trenches of negative emotions, your energy takes a nosedive. Now, this might not be groundbreaking stuff, but bear with me for a second because there's a deeper layer to this.

Dr Hawkins uncovered something truly captivating about the emotion of bravery. He found that 'courage' was the pivotal emotion, the one that marked the shift from negativity to positivity in our consciousness. He described it as the gateway to empowerment, asserting that, at this level, life could take on an entirely different hue.

Bravery dissolves negative emotions.

At the lower rungs of consciousness, the world can seem too bleak to overcome, filled with hopelessness, sadness, fear or frustration. Every single person I've ever coached has danced with negative emotions like these at some point in their lives – it's just a part of the human experience. But, while it's crucial to acknowledge and feel the full spectrum of emotions, we don't want to set up camp in the land of negativity because, when we linger there too long, those low energies can drag us down like quicksand, and keep us there. It can feel so bad sometimes, that even the thought of pulling yourself out of that negative funk can feel like scaling a mountain.

Bravery gives us access to positive emotions.

According to Hawkins, at the level of courage, life becomes an adventure, a thrill ride brimming with excitement, challenge and stimulation. When we consciously choose bravery – which is synonymous with courage and holds the same emotion – everything changes. We need bravery to overcome our negative states; it's the *bridging* emotion that gives us access to more positive emotions. It's like stepping into a whole new realm of possibility and vitality.

So, what's the game plan?

It's simple: take back the reins; you're the one in the driver's seat.

How to take back the reins

How do we take control of our emotional state when we are going through a break-up, feeling overwhelmed at work or lacking purpose in our lives?

Well, you need to take a little step forward that begins to shift your emotional landscape, a *Little Brave Act*. It could be as simple as taking a deep breath and choosing to let go of resentment. Or it could be extending forgiveness, even when it feels impossible. Such brave acts may seem insignificant at first, but they're the building blocks of transformation, paving the way for a gradual ascent from anger and despair to acceptance, and ultimately, to the radiant joy waiting on the other side.

Every act of bravery starts with a single step.

How many times have we been told, 'Just slap on a smile, find your joy, and take care of yourself'? While there is wisdom in these words and self-care and mindfulness can work wonders, let's be real here: happiness isn't something we can conjure up on command. It's not like flipping a switch. If self-care and mindfulness are not already a part of our daily routine, if they're not ingrained in our habits, then starting them will take courage. It will take a *Little Brave Act* to begin.

Bravery isn't just a nice addition to our emotional toolkit; it's the very foundation we need to build upon. Dr David Hawkins' research showed us that bravery isn't just a stepping stone; it's the gateway to a whole spectrum of positive emotions.

One of the biggest mistakes we can make is thinking that life doesn't ask *us* to be brave. We tell ourselves that bravery is for other people. But here's the raw truth: the human experience demands bravery from *all* of us at some point. No one gets a free pass.

Mentally strong people *expect* adversity. They know that challenges in life are a given, not an exception. If we remain unprepared for challenges, we will quickly fall into a victim mindset when they arise. Whereas those with a brave mindset know that life is going to put us through challenges, trials and unexpected shocks; and they see these as potentials for transformation.

Why little acts, not big?

'Sometimes the smallest step in the right direction
ends up being the biggest step of your life.
Tiptoe if you must, but take the step.'

– NAEEM CALLAWAY

When we have big dreams, we often believe we need to take massive, grandiose actions to realise them. We think we have to make these gigantic leaps to transform our lives. But here's the thing: size is an illusion. Some of the most powerful elements on earth are tiny. Think about an acorn – small and unassuming, yet it holds the potential to grow into a mighty oak tree. Or building a muscle – it takes time and consistency to build a muscle. It's not about the size of our actions; it's about their impact. It's about those small, consistent steps, those *Little Brave Acts*, that build up over time and create real, lasting change. It's not about moving mountains all at once.

Brave acts can be small, quiet and invisible.

You can't expect to jump straight from anger to joy; it's just too big a jump. Think about it: when you're seething with anger, your emotions are at their peak intensity; there's a raging storm inside you. Now, imagine trying to skip over all that turmoil to experience joy – it would be like trying to cross a wide chasm between two states of being without a bridge!

What if you're drowning in a sea of despair and hopelessness? Picture yourself trying to propel your body from the depth of that despair all the way up into a world of sunshine and rainbows with a single stroke. That would defy logic. It simply would not be possible. Our only option would be to muster one small stroke at a time. So don't worry about making a giant leap out of the darkness. You don't need to see the whole path to the surface, you just need to take the next stroke. That's how we swim our way back to the surface, one brave stroke at a time. Real-life bravery is rarely about taking a single, big heroic act. It is about taking one little step and then another.

Too often we wait to feel brave before we leap, so we never leap, or wait too long and someone pushes us. In reality, you are not likely to feel brave before you start. All *Little Brave Acts* are birthed from an experience of fear. Commonly it is paralysing, terrifying, nail-gripping fear. So feeling brave in that moment may well feel impossible.

Before your Little Brave Act, *bravery will feel like fear.*

But we need to act anyway, take that first small step, because this small action generates the feeling of bravery. Only when the *Little Brave Act* is done will you feel the emotion of bravery. Don't wait to feel brave. Take the step first, and bravery will follow.

You may only feel brave after your Little Brave Act.

When being brave is the only thing you can control

'The question of life being fair or unfair is one of the first things to drop away once you truly understand that you're as vulnerable as the next person to life's vagaries.'

– LEIGH SALES, *ANY ORDINARY DAY*

That need to act brave before feeling brave is never more important than when we are faced with catastrophic change – those times when life rips the rug out from under us, when the ground beneath us shifts suddenly and we're left feeling like we're free-falling into the abyss. Like when you lose someone you love, and the weight of that loss feels unbearable, pressing down on your chest. When your partner is struck by a sudden illness, and you're thrust into the role of caretaker without a roadmap. Or watching your financial stability vanish in an instant due to a cryptocurrency crash, leaving you to wonder how you'll pay the bills next month. Then there are natural disasters – the sheer terror of watching your home burn to the ground as a bushfire engulfs everything you've built.

It's as if the universe has taken your life and tossed it around like confetti in the wind. In these moments, when everything feels like it's spinning out of control, the only thing you can control is what you do next. It might be letting the tears flow freely, allowing yourself to feel and release the overwhelm. It might be reaching out to a friend for support, or as simple as choosing to get out of bed and face the day.

Bravery becomes an anchor, steadying us. It's the quiet strength we summon when the ground beneath us gives way, when we're forced to navigate a new reality we never saw coming. It's the determination to take one step forward, even when it feels like the world is crumbling around us. Bravery is the whisper in our hearts that says, 'You can do this,' even when every other part of us is filled with doubt.

Caroline's powerful little step: when bravery is a calling

'Life shrinks or expands in proportion to one's courage.'

– RYAN HOLIDAY, *COURAGE IS CALLING*

Bravery can sometimes feel like a calling, a whisper from your soul urging you to act. In that moment, your sole purpose is to take any little step – one *Little Brave Act* that sparks the momentum of change desperately needed in your life. You'll recognise that you have postponed change for far too long, and now is the time to summon your courage and move forward.

A client of mine, Caroline, had been married for 16 years. She had created the life she'd dreamed about and it looked exactly as she imagined it would when she was younger. She was a mother of four boys and had built and designed her ideal house. Her Plan A was in place. And yet, it felt like anything but a dream come true. It felt lonely, false and small. She knew she had to leave the marriage, yet couldn't. She was torn between the familiarity of what was and the uncertainty of what could be.

Why do we not leave until every cell in our body is beckoning us to go? I have worked with many clients like Caroline and have stood in similar shoes myself. We hang in there because the shame, pain and guilt of leaving is unbearable. We don't want to admit our Plan A has failed. And to compound the weight of emotions, we truly believe it's all our fault. We stay, thinking we can fix the relationship and, worse still, we believe we are responsible for doing the fixing. Why? Because in that moment, we believe that we are the source of the problem.

This is not just true of marriages. I have had terrible jobs I stayed in, thinking, 'I am failing at delivering, I need to work harder.' I have outgrown friendships where I have maintained the connection, believing, 'I am not a good friend, I need to try harder.' I have continued pursuing academic degrees that no longer inspired me, convinced, 'I need to finish this; I need to try harder to find the passion again.'

Eventually, Caroline knew with every cell in her body that it was simply time to go. 'It felt like a calling to leave,' she explained. She had no plan for after she left, nothing thought out; there was no convenient time to leave, but she had become aware that leaving was simply her only purpose in that moment.

For Caroline, as for many of my clients, taking *any* little step towards starting a new life is brave, and necessary, if you want to create change.

Bravery is a quiet, steady resolve to keep moving forward.

When I've worked with clients, they often describe their *Little Brave Acts* as undeniable nudges from within, urging them to take that initial step towards transformation. It's that moment when updating your resume doesn't just seem like a task, but a powerful act of reclaiming your career path. It's opening a journal to confront the raw emotions surrounding a relationship at a crossroads. It's reaching out to another mother in your circle when the challenges of newborn parenthood seem overwhelming. It's switching off from mindless scrolling on social media to give yourself a break from unhelpful comparisons. It's saying no to that glass of wine you know will muddy your thinking. These acts, however small they may seem, resonate as a profound and urgent calling.

When bravery is messy

'You can choose courage, or you can choose comfort, but you cannot choose both.'

– BRENÉ BROWN

Sometimes bravery can feel more like a desperate response to an intolerable situation than a conscious calling, and it can be emotionally messy. I experienced this myself as I was driving to the launch of my first book and ugly-crying the whole way – tears streaming down my face like I was trying to win an Oscar for Best Meltdown. You see, I had recently broken up with a man I thought I loved, our relationship quickly turning from fairytale to cautionary tale.

I was supposed to strut into that event like the protagonist of a bestseller – successful, radiant and in a relationship so dreamy it would make Nicholas Sparks blush. I had envisioned a red carpet with photographers snapping busily away.

Instead, reality handed me a banana peel and smudged mascara. Looking back, I'm glad it did, but at the time, it wasn't pretty.

For months prior, I had received a multitude of signs that this relationship needed to end. It was like the universe had been sending me an excessive number of celestial emojis just to tell me, 'Break up and let the stars finally align for you.' But, true to my form, I was intent on reshuffling my oracle deck until, 38 shuffles later, I pulled the card I wanted that said, 'Yes! Stay, he is your soulmate.'

I *wanted* it to be him. I needed it to be. I was already in my 40s and my biological clock was waving a red flag. I *thought* he was my last chance at achieving my Plan A – marriage, then kids, naturally conceived.

Ignoring all the signs, I eventually got sick. I had a migraine that wouldn't go away and a period that lasted three weeks – my womb was crying. Living your life with your head and not your heart will do that. I should have taken my physical pain as a warning that I was not living my best life, even with all the excitement of my book launch approaching!

Eventually, two weeks before the launch, I sat on the edge of my bed, my stomach in knots, and unknowingly took my first little step into a *Little Brave Act*: I asked myself brave questions requiring dangerous answers.

Why dangerous? Because if I answered such questions with complete honesty, I knew things would change in my life, and that things were likely to get worse before they got better.

My brave questions included:

- Can this person really give me what I want?
- Am I the best version of me when I am with him?
- Do I bring out the best version of him?
- Can I live with this level of anxiety in my life and achieve my purpose work?
- Why am I so scared of being alone?
- Can I handle the shame of being older and single?
- Can I handle telling everyone about yet another break-up?

When I answered these questions with courage and honesty, I found clarity. That same day we broke up. It felt like a *brave* break-up. I was clear, firm, willing to sit in the messy uncomfortable process that would follow and to stick to my guns. No one likes it when their plan fails, but I had to face this failure head-on, even if it did jeopardise my ability to conceive and have children. I owed it to myself to be happy first. The universe wanted me to be happy first.

Resisting the pull to the past

'From little things big things grow.'

– PAUL KELLY AND KEV CARMODY

You might be thinking, Sheila, ending that relationship was a *big* brave act, not a *little* act. But it was in fact made up of many *Little Brave Acts*. We had broken up countless times, and so my first *Little Brave Act* was finding a way to stick with my decision every day, face my failed Plan A and not go back to him, like I had so many times before. I started by collecting all of his things from around my house. He hadn't quite been living with me – it was a 'situationship'; still, I opened every drawer, every closet and scanned every bookshelf, and piled his belongings in a box by my doorway. My next *Little Brave Act* was texting him to pick everything up. Previously when

I had broken up and become scared of being alone, I'd always reverted to my old self, too quickly.

Our pasts have a strong gravitational pull, drawing us back to the familiar and safe. Can you relate to this, wanting to step back into your comfort zone? Break-ups, finding a new job after a redundancy, recovering after financial loss, finding new meaning in life after the death of a loved one – anything and everything we want to achieve will always take a series of small acts forward that require the courage to do things differently this time.

Being brave is never convenient or comfortable. We need to accept that the process of taking *Little Brave Acts* will be messy as painful emotions are stirred up. Searching for a new job post-redundancy, each application and interview demands resilience in the face of potential rejection. Financial setbacks may require the discomfort of re-evaluating our spending habits and making tough decisions. Our way forward through grief may see us dissolving in tears in front of complete strangers.

After you take your first *Little Brave Act*, the next one is a little easier. And the next. But each step forward does not make you immune from uncertainty. Two weeks after I split with my boyfriend, I arrived at my book launch feeling somewhat fragile. When the audience had settled, I started to speak in a voice that was hesitant yet determined. I decided to scrap my over-rehearsed, scripted speech, and instead speak authentically about the messiness of bravery, and how bravery is often small, quiet and inconvenient, and sometimes not social media friendly. I knew my message was landing because more and more people in the audience began to nod. Many friends and clients in the audience knew I was being brave by just standing there and speaking my truth – their truth too. Bravery is doing the things you are scared to do, and sometimes having an audience witnessing you doing it. They felt brave for me in the moment, even though I felt like a sacred and vulnerable little girl.

The details of the rest of my book launch are a blur, lost in the fog of that break-up. My memory decided to take a spontaneous vacation right when I was supposed to be basking in success. Faces, conversations and champagne toasts are all jumbled together, obscured by the emotional haze that accompanied the end of that chapter in my personal life.

You will most likely not feel brave, when you are doing the bravest thing.

There's always this part of our heart that clings desperately to the familiar, to the comfort of what we've always known. I implore you to embrace the messiness of bravery, even when every fibre of your being resists and whispers, 'I don't want to be brave; I just want things to stay as they are.' It's a paradoxical dance between yearning for stability and the necessity to change. In these moments, the hardest battles are clearly not fought against external forces, but within ourselves — an internal struggle between the security of what is and the messy uncertainty of what could be.

This is why your mindset is so important. As a coach, I've had the privilege of witnessing the magic of clients pivoting into a brave mindset, time and time again. When we tap into a brave mindset, we unlock the ability to take *Little Brave Acts*, regardless of the challenge we're experiencing and its level of difficulty. We understand that life throws curveballs, and that we need to dig deep for grit and resilience. We cut out the energy-draining drama and fiercely guard our own healing path. And, regardless of the challenge we're facing, we actually find gratitude in that moment. A brave mindset is the game-changing attitude that can transform us from victim to victor, and it starts with understanding that challenges will always come, that plans will always fail, and so we will always have to be brave and rethink them.

Brave truths

- Bravery is not always about big leaps of courage. Brave acts can be small, quiet and seemingly insignificant steps - moments of bravery that pave the way for greatness.

- Bravery is the pivotal emotion that shifts our consciousness from negative to positive. Knowing this we can change our emotional state instantly thought a *Little Brave Act*.

- You will most likely not feel brave when you are doing the bravest thing.

- You may only feel brave after doing your *Little Brave Act*. Acting *through* fear is the only way we can feel brave.

- People with a brave mindset expect adversity and are prepared and ready to be brave.

Brave questions

- What small act of courage could you undertake today that would bring you one step closer to your dreams or personal goals?

- Can you identify a fear that's been holding you back? What's one small way you could begin to confront this fear?

- Reflect on a time when you felt genuinely proud of yourself. What brave choice did you make to create that moment?

- If you could achieve one thing without the risk of failure, what would it be? How does that guide you towards your next *Little Brave Act?*

- Who in your life embodies the bravery you admire? What can you learn from their actions that you can apply in your own life this week?

Brave mantra

I take *Little Brave Acts* daily.

PART 2
Letting go

CHAPTER 2

The powerful little step of failing

'The secret of life is to fall seven times and to get up eight times.'

– PAULO COELHO

When I wrote *Brave: Courageously Live Your Truth*, I did not realise that I would have to step into the bravest version of myself in the years following. I became a 'lab rat' for the message I was called to share, and tested in many ways to make sure that the message was robust and durable. At that point, I still assumed that every plan I devised would work out fine, as long as I planned them with bravery. I hadn't yet acknowledged that most initial plans inevitably fail, because they are often created from the wrong stuff or we simply outgrow them. This was true for me, especially in my personal life.

After the book launch my motivational speaking career gained momentum and a beautiful phenomenon unfolded: attendees began sharing with me, through social media and personal emails, the little things they were doing to take a step forward in their lives. They were, in essence sharing their *Little Brave Acts*. When this started to happen, I knew I had the simmering of a movement in which the foundation lay in thinking bravely, and the subsequent steps involved in acting bravely.

I saw myself as brave, especially in my professional life. I was fearless when it came to quitting, pivoting, and diving headfirst into new projects and jobs that felt right in my bones. That's how I found my way to a purpose-filled career that sang to my soul, leveraging my passions and talents in ways that felt both powerful and true. But here's the thing: my bravery was selective. It was convenient bravery.

In my personal life, I was the complete opposite of brave. I had a chorus line of romantic relationships behind me, which I could only describe as toxic; though later I realised that it was *my* toxic mind and low expectations that had created disappointment after disappointment. I didn't have the courage to leave when I should have. I wore loyalty like it was a badge of honour in relationships that drained me. I needed *Little Brave Acts* to drop my victim mentality, to rebuild my self-love and ask myself the courageous question: 'What am I doing to attract this?'

I wanted a family. My biological clock was like a relentless jackhammer in my head. The thought of delaying love felt like I was putting off having a child, and honestly, that terrified me. I was trapped in this mental loop, thinking that every minute I waited was just another minute slipping away.

I couldn't fathom the Plan A for my personal life failing. If I didn't get married and have kids in my 30s, then what? The question I was not ready to ask, but needed to, was *'Why am I so attached to this plan?'*

How we plan

When we have an idea, there is an energy that bubbles up from within. It's as if a wellspring of inspiration gushes forth, overflowing with possibilities. Creating our Plan A in this moment is easy; it's almost instinctual. We know exactly what we want to achieve and we're hell-bent on making it happen – channelling all our energies into supporting this plan at all costs. For me that was get married young, have kids and live happily ever after. For others, it might be climbing the corporate ladder to a coveted corner office, launching a dream business that magically takes off without a hitch, or travelling the world in search of adventure and enlightenment. We paint these vivid pictures of what life should look like, convinced that if we just follow the steps, everything will fall into place.

We don't just have relationship plans, we have plans about everything in life: career aspirations, the academic path we will pursue, when we want to have children, the exotic destinations we dream of exploring during a gap year, the savings we need to buy our first home. And plans come in various timelines – long-term, medium-term and short-term. With a plan, it's like navigating with a reliable compass and map, a guiding system to lead us towards the holy grail of success, fulfilment and abundance. Our plans make us feel like the masters of our destiny. We cling to them with unwavering dedication. Even if those plans are made of the wrong stuff, and no amount of bravery will make them work, we persist like someone trying to assemble IKEA furniture without instructions.

Why?

The security of Plan A

'Man plans, and God laughs.'

– YIDDISH PROVERB

To most people, plans are more than just blueprints for our lives. They are the stories we tell ourselves, narratives that give our days purpose and meaning. My traditional Plan A – to marry and conceive naturally – was one such story. I believed it held the secret to a life well-lived, that it represented the pinnacle of personal success. I clung to it because society told me to, and because managing my life this way reassured me I was on the right track. In my mind, it was a *good* plan.

Plan As give us the illusion of control. We all seek to command the tides of fate with our perfectly organised to-do lists and jam-packed timetables. But here's the deal: life has a way of throwing curveballs that leave our plans in tatters. We're left standing there, wondering why we ever thought we could control it all. You see, the truth is: total control is just an illusion. It's a comforting story we tell ourselves until it's shattered by the unexpected.

This is not to say we don't have any control. That is far from the message here. A wise friend once told me that we can only control the controllable. I'm sure you've had a few people relinquish that gem of wisdom on you! It's obvious, right? Obvious yet amazing how much we need to remind ourselves of its truth, and even more amazing how many times in life we find ourselves painstakingly tied up in knots trying to control the uncontrollable.

Here's another interesting thing about plans: we rarely recognise that we ever had a Plan A until it crumbles before us. Up until that point, it's simply The Plan. It's the one and only plan, the foolproof plan that makes us feel invincible, giving us a sense of a certainty about the direction in which our life is headed. The plan builds up our self-esteem. It gives our parents and friends certainty that we are growing up nicely and obediently. In many ways, the plan serves as a safety net.

And lastly, we believe that all plans are permanent. We may not allow ourselves to see beyond our initial plan. The future seems too far off, or it may seem inconceivable that the chapter that we are in will, and must, eventually end, to allow for a new chapter to begin. The mindset of denial can and will prevent us from growing and evolving.

In his book *Transitions: Making Sense of Life's Changes*, William Bridges highlights that every transition begins with an ending. He writes, 'We resist transition not because we can't accept change, but because we can't accept letting go of that piece of our lives that gave us our identity.' This insight highlights the difficulty we all face in moving beyond our initial plans and embracing new possibilities.

When Plan A fails

'Failure is the condiment that gives success its flavor.'

– TRUMAN CAPOTE

But what if the plan is wrong for us? What if it is *supposed* to fail?

There are two main reasons why our Plan As need to fail. The first is that our Plan A was never right for us. We need it to fail so we can be free of it. It is a course correction nudging us onto our true path. These initial plans aren't really *ours* – they're borrowed scripts handed down to us by parents, culture or peer groups. That's why so many Plan As don't quite pan out. They often carry the weight of who we think we *should* be, shaped by societal and familial expectations. It's like we have been handed a role in a play – one that we never auditioned for, but took on anyway.

We go to great lengths to fit in, don't we?

Maybe we stayed in a soul-sucking job because it looked good on paper, or we stuck it out in a relationship that suffocated our true self because we were afraid of being alone. Perhaps we chased a career that impressed everyone else, ignoring the quiet whispers of our real passions. Or we forced ourselves into social circles that didn't resonate, pretending to enjoy interests just to fit in with outgrown friendships, losing sight of what we genuinely care about.

Our Plan A needs to fail because it's the only way our lives can truly progress. There comes a time when the cozy sweater becomes scratchy, the happiness wanes, and we're left with a choice: to stay in the safety of our stagnant, comfortable existence or to summon the courage to leap into the unknown. That's when we need to acknowledge that what got us to this point won't necessarily get us to where we want to go next. It's time to move from the comfort zone into the growth zone of our lives, to shed the old skins and step boldly onto our true paths.

Plan A needs to fail so we can find our true path.

Let's also be honest about the resistance we often feel when transitioning between various stages of life. Picture the shift from single life to marriage, where the fairytale romance clashes with the gritty reality after the honeymoon period wears off, revealing cracks you never saw coming. Or the jump into motherhood, where the perfect birth plan disintegrates amid the chaos of labour and the relentless demands of newborn parenting. Then there's the gut-wrenching empty-nest syndrome, when your identity as a parent feels like it's evaporating, leaving you to face a hollow silence. And menopause, when your body, once familiar, now feels like a stranger, forcing you to confront changes that shake you to your core.

Bruce Feiler, in *Life is in the Transitions: Mastering Change at Any Age*, emphasises that life is a series of nonlinear transitions.

He writes, 'Life is the story you tell yourself. And your story is not a straight line; it's a complex and ever-changing narrative.'

Each of these transitions can shatter Plan A, showing us that life's true path often lies beyond our neatly laid plans.

But it's not all doom and gloom. These transitions hold within them the seeds of transformation, of renewal, and the opportunity to emerge stronger and wiser than ever before. Here's the thing: if we don't take the little step of letting go of the safety and security of our old life, the universe will step in with some tough love and ensure that our Plan A fails, and quite often in a spectacular fashion. A voice then whispers in our ear, 'Sweetheart, you're not meant to play small.' This is the much-needed push to step forward on our path.

Caroline's powerful little step: accepting failure

'It's going to be okay in the end. If it's not okay, it's not the end.'

– ANON

When my client Caroline, who felt the calling to be brave, allowed her Plan A to fail, she also discovered previously unknown possibilities. She found the self-esteem, courage and resources to leave her marriage.

'The whole time I had thought that *I* was the problem,' she told me. 'So, at the same time as I was throwing my energy into saving my marriage, I went deeply into my own work. This ended up being my saviour because the more I worked on myself, I realised it *wasn't* just me. I was only 50 percent of the problem, even though my husband was telling me that I was 100 percent of the problem.'

Caroline's voice is the voice of so many of us. Women commonly don't like to take up space – unless it comes to blame and guilt, then we will happily shoulder more than our fair share. We are gold medal winners in carrying that burden! But when we start doing the inner work, we can realise that while we must take 100 percent responsibility for our actions, we are only 50 percent of the equation within a marriage.

'He told me I'd never leave,' Caroline told me. 'Maybe because he felt that I didn't have anyone to financially support me. I didn't have a job. I needed him, and so I had no boundaries in the marriage.'

She reflected, 'I often questioned how I would convince the children that I'd done the right thing, when I had to take them out of the family home I'd built. But then part of me was also saying, well, I'm not actually teaching my children what a relationship should look like, either.'

In that moment, Caroline started to become open to her next *Little Brave Act*. The possibility of another life. One she had never considered before; one without the perfect family home and nuclear family. One she wouldn't have even considered if she hadn't stepped bravely into a new perspective. She emerged feeling wiser and more resilient than ever before, and that she would become a better role model for her children.

The gift of failure

'Failure is not the opposite of success; it's part of success.'

– ARIANNA HUFFINGTON

Failure is a sacred teacher, guiding us towards the essence of our true selves. When we stumble and fall, we aren't losing our way; we're gaining wisdom. John C. Maxwell, in *Failing Forward*, reminds us that, 'The difference between average people and achieving people is their perception of and response to failure.' Failure becomes a sort of soul curriculum, revealing our strengths and vulnerabilities in equal measure. In the dance of setbacks, we learn to trust the messy beautiful process of becoming. Success isn't just about reaching a destination; it's about embracing the journey with all its falls and rises, recognising that failure isn't an endpoint, but a transformative chapter in the story of our unfolding selves.

Failure is a teacher, not a tragedy.

Even though we know that failing is good for us, it still hurts. Really hurts.

These moments of personal reckoning can be the most transformative experiences in our lives, yet we don't see them that way initially – because they weren't in our original plan. After we overcome the challenges they bring, we can often look back and realise they were an opportunity to reassess, pivot and maybe even discover the existence of other paths, other plans, waiting to unfold. They were an invitation to embrace the uncertainty of life and to recognise that sometimes beauty and growth come not from adhering to the original plan, but from following unexpected detours.

Still, it can take great effort to step into the failure of our initial plans. When life throws us something unforeseen and we have to be tough, flexible or change our plans, it often catches us off guard.

It's like there's this important lesson missing in our education system. We are taught algebra over adaptability, cursive writing over curiosity, trigonometry over tenacity. So we end up having to teach ourselves about failure as we grow older.

The cool part is that, as adults, we *can* become our own teachers. We *can* learn to handle the unexpected, adapt and find strength in tough times. Megan McArdle, in *The Up Side of Down*, emphasises that, 'The key to success is not avoiding failure but learning how to fail well.' She elaborates on the idea that failure, when approached with the right mindset, can be a powerful catalyst for personal and professional growth. McArdle argues, 'The ability to fail well – to adapt, to recover, and to learn from our mistakes – is what separates those who ultimately succeed from those who give up.'

Our next *Litte Brave Act* is to accept that Plan A will always fail, in some shape or form. But if we can embrace failure and deal with the emotional fallout effectively, great opportunities await.

Brave truths

- We must be brave in all areas of our lives. Not selectively brave.

- Plan As will always fail, because they were never truly ours.

- Plan As can fail in many different ways - because we outgrow them, because they do not allow us to be our authentic self, and because there is a bigger plan for our life beyond Plan A.

- If we want real control we must drop the illusion of control.

- Your failure is not *in the way* of your success. Failure is *on the way* to your success.

Brave questions

- Can you reflect on a past 'perfect' plan that failed, but then that failure resulted in a better yet unexpected opportunity presenting itself?

- In what areas of your life can you start embracing uncertainty more?

- Can you acknowledge a time in your past where letting go of a failing Plan A led you closer to your authentic self and true desires?

- Did you eventually feel relieved that your Plan A in the past failed? This question should reveal where you have been compromising yourself.

- Are there aspects of your life where you have been in your comfort zone for too long? Are you ready for growth in those parts of your life?

Brave mantra

I surrender to the greater plan of my life.

CHAPTER 3

The powerful little step of embracing shame

'Shame is a soul-eating emotion.'

– C.G. JUNG

Before we can embrace the opportunities that failure provides, we need to deal with the emotional fallout that can leave us paralysed. And there is nothing quite like the feeling of shame to derail us.

Shame is often the first emotion we face when plans fail. Our fear of failure is, in many ways, a fear of shame. We all run from the excruciating, painful, debilitating experience of shame. This is part of human nature. Shame rattles our self-worth to the core, making us feel like we can't even face the day ahead. When we experience shame, we often use words like 'wanting to die' or 'hide.' Sometimes, just getting out of bed becomes an insurmountable task.

I've known the deafening roar of shame many times, from experiencing the sting of redundancy – leaving the office with a meagre box of belongings and my cheeks burning, to the heartbreak of infidelity as I walked in on an unfaithful partner. I've stumbled over words while speaking on stage, feeling exposed and inadequate. And there was the shame of turning up at my book launch alone.

I've also known the quieter types of shame – the kind that comes with being single and childless on my 40th birthday or walking down the aisle as a bridesmaid for my younger sisters, while deflecting the persistent questions about my own turn to wed. I felt it too as I masked my struggles of isolation during the pandemic, despite battling a loneliness that threatened to consume me. Shame like this can be concealed with a smile, a touch of red lipstick and a fabulous frock. But putting on a brave face is not the same as being brave. I was only fooling myself.

A brave face is not the same as being brave.

I've witnessed firsthand how shame can act as a formidable barrier to my clients' progress too.

Shame is the heavy burden of explaining to family that you are leaving your husband because he hit you. Shame is the silent suffering of infertility. Shame is the weight of unfulfilled dreams and unanswered prayers. It's the discomfort of receiving your salary package and feeling the need to negotiate for higher pay. It's the acute embarrassment of your toddler throwing a tantrum at a party, and the judgmental stares of onlookers burning into your soul. It's the guilt of not wanting to celebrate your pay rise when your friends are struggling around you, for fear of being perceived as boastful or insensitive.

Shame is the difficulty of speaking up for what you desire sexually in the bedroom, a fear of rejection and ridicule overshadowing your desires. It's the loneliness of not having plans on New Year's Eve, with the pressure to conform to societal expectations of celebration and revelry.

Shame is the struggle of not losing the baby weight, with the relentless pressure to conform to unrealistic beauty standards; or the frustration of struggling with perimenopausal symptoms, only to be told by doctors that you're not menopausal. It's the invalidation of your experiences, and the dismissal of your pain and suffering.

Shame is yet another relationship failure that you don't want to admit to friends and family, so you persist with it – right up until your book launch!

What all these examples have in common is the presence of an audience, real or imagined, watching and judging us in these vulnerable moments. We internalise society's expectations of what a successful, social media-friendly and happy life looks like, and when we perceive ourselves as falling short, shame takes hold.

In those moments, shame silences us. It compels us to lie about our situation, to pretend that we're doing okay, or even happy – when in reality, we're miserable and lost. We feel a deep sense of self-disgust, trapped in a downward shame spiral that threatens to consume us. And yet, despite our inner turmoil, we betray ourselves, agreeing with the values and viewpoints of others, telling ourselves that we'll do better – even though we know we're at our limit.

Keeping secrets

'Shame thrives in silence and darkness, but loses its power in the light of honesty and vulnerability.'

– TAHIRA KASHYAP, *NO SHAME*

Back in the middle of 2014, I found myself staring at my wardrobe wondering what sassy suit to wear that day. For many years, I had been obsessed with developing my career and had invested thousands of dollars in looking the part. My wardrobe offered quite the choice, but it had been three weeks since I'd worn a suit and stiletto heels. The corns on my toes had started to heal, the soles of my feet were feeling softer, and my hair was healthier, as I had been wearing my natural curl instead of straightening it daily. Yet my eyes welled up with the weight of shame, because it had been three weeks since I lost my job.

It was a job I had known I needed to leave, but the fear of lacking the security of an income and the pressure to conform had kept me tethered to a life that no longer served me. For years I had been saying I wanted to start my own spiritual healing business, but the familiar chorus of limiting beliefs held me back:

'I'll never make enough money.'

'What will my parents say?'

'People don't respect spiritual healers.'

Such thoughts, born out of fear and shame, had kept me trapped in a cycle of unhappiness and self-doubt. At the same time, they had kept me safe and in my comfort zone. I had given much energy and time to these thoughts, further cementing them within my thinking, allowing them to recur every day with ease. They reassured me that my Plan A was *the* Plan.

That day I was due to meet my sister for lunch. She was flying in from overseas for a brief visit and we had arranged to meet in the city on my lunchbreak. The problem was that I didn't have a job in the city anymore, thus I didn't have a lunchbreak, and I hadn't told her or anyone in my family that I had lost my job. The shame was too debilitating. When anyone phoned me, I would make up a story about my day. And now I was planning to travel into the city in a suit to pretend I still had a job!

Secrets and dishonesty are the hallmarks of shame-based behaviour, and here I was living them daily. I was dishonest with myself and with those around me.

Shame expert Brené Brown defines shame as 'the intensely painful feeling or experience of believing that we are flawed and therefore unworthy of love, belonging, and connection.'

I come from a conservative culture whose values were based on not only having a job, but a great job with an important job title. Success did not involve following passion, but profit. I felt like I was not allowed to belong to myself, I had to belong to the clan. Thus, I always felt my individual thoughts were wrong, as they strayed too far from what was acceptable. This was how shame showed up for me daily.

But the universe had had enough of watching me live my life with my head and not my heart. My heart was breaking daily, and so the universe was going to save me.

As I was sitting on my bed that day, feeling yet another wave of shame wash over me, time suspended for a moment and a new voice entered my mind. The voice said, 'Isn't it time you were free of this lie? Isn't it time you got on with making the changes in your life that you really want?'

Caroline's powerful little step: the pain of shame

'I didn't fight or shame my thoughts, I questioned them, and they stopped shaming me.'

– BYRON KATIE

My client Caroline also suffered great shame as her Plan A was failing.

'When I realised my dream of being married and having the perfect family with the perfect house was dissolving,' she told me, 'I felt like a complete failure. I think I held onto my marriage because I didn't want to fail. I felt like I had failed as a wife and a mother because I had tried everything possible to make it work. I ticked almost every single box of the things you need to do before you leave a marriage. We went to counselling; we sold the house and went travelling around Australia to work on the marriage – we even moved interstate.'

I remember nodding as Caroline told me this. For so many women, just knowing that they had tried everything can provide a sense of peace later, when the weight of guilt would press down heavily on them.

Caroline reflected, 'I carried a devastating feeling of shame every day. Deep shame, deep guilt. To the outside world, we had looked like a perfect family. I almost didn't want that bubble to burst because I thought, the more I believed the façade, the less I needed to change. I was fooling myself.'

I asked Caroline what inspired her decision to finally leave.

She responded, 'I couldn't take the pain anymore. I was prepared to take a shot at uncertainty; and I hate uncertainty. I realised that moving out of our family home and this marriage *had* to be less painful than where I was with the certainty of my current life.'

Living with shame over time becomes more and more tiring. It will slowly drain us of energy and clarity. A week later Caroline left.

Overcoming shame

'Shame hates it when we reach out and tell our story. It hates having words wrapped around it – it can't survive being shared.'

– BRENÉ BROWN

If we lack the tools to face and process shame, we end up retracing our steps back to our earlier plan, even when the universe is beckoning us towards a different path. We return to unhealthy relationships, shelve our side hustles and revert to corporate jobs, or seek solace in self-medication, self-flagellation and self-denial. Shame has the power to keep us stuck if we let it.

Shame is the emotion we draw on to
ensure we remain safe and hidden.

At some point, the only way past it is to rise up against it.

My hand trembled as I picked up the phone to call my sister. She answered, and I started confessing. It was a one-way outpouring; I needed to get out what I was going through. I allowed myself to be vulnerable with her in a way that I had never been before.

We can process our shame on the other
side of a brave conversation.

To my surprise, she listened with compassion and empathy, acknowledging that it was time for me to make changes. While she didn't understand everything I said, she was distressed to see me in this much pain and shared this with me.

When bravery and vulnerability meet, a space of love, compassion and empathy opens up. But most importantly, this is the place where change begins.

After the conversation with my sister, I finally found the energy to think clearly about my future. I started my side hustle the following day – branding, website design, dreaming about my new career. I won't pretend that the next five months of starting my business were easy, but there was a spring in my step, and momentum for my life's new direction started to build.

More importantly, when I look back at the scared woman who wanted to pretend she was employed and get on a train to meet her sister in the city for lunch, I have compassion for her. I respect her tenacity to be resourceful and to go to such extremes because she cared so much about what her family thought and needed to belong. I have found that shaming our shame only keeps us stuck.

My powerful little step of calling my sister moved me into a newer version of myself that was able to experience new healthier thoughts, new healthier feelings and a new life.

Forgiving myself for wanting to hide and pretend was also a small act of bravery.

This journey of learning, growing, healing, and evolving is not linear. It is messy, unpredictable and often fraught with challenges. But perhaps therein lies the beauty of it all. The process of growth often begins with shame and ends with bravery. It is through our willingness to confront our deepest fears and vulnerabilities that we discover the strength and resilience that lie within us, waiting to be unleashed. And as I continued on my journey, I did so with a new-found sense of purpose and determination, knowing that each little step would bring me one step closer to becoming the person I was always meant to be.

Can we accept that moving from shame to bravery is a common part of the process.

Hiding our shame

'Shame thrives in secrecy but shrinks in the light of empathy.'

– KRISTIN NEFF

I hid my fertility shame for years, even though I knew I was reaching my limits. I had wanted to meet someone special, settle down, marry and conceive kids naturally. But year after year, relationship after relationship, I had watched my initial plan for my romantic life slip further and further away. But back in my late 30s, I had instigated a potential backup. If my initial Plan A *was* going to fail, I'd make damn sure I had a substitute plan – I would put my eggs on ice, ready for the perfect day. Oh, how I love a plan! Who doesn't?

I froze my eggs. What else could I do *but* freeze my eggs and wait for the right person? I couldn't possibly have a child alone! That would be even more shameful than waiting, I thought. Little did I know how far shame was yet to push me.

Shame sits in the heartache of not having children and the constant reminders of what society deems as the pinnacle of success and fulfilment. If you can't reach those peaks, on time and in a certain way, you feel shame at your failure. Women's fertility struggles are usually very private and solitary affairs. We speak in whispers about them, or perhaps don't share them with anyone at all. We instead find ourselves engrossed in Instagram reels, following the journey of the 'brave few' who document their experiences with egg freezing, IVF and non-traditional conception methods, until they themselves become fatigued, disillusioned and burned out. We are not only at war with Mother Nature, but the apparent natural order of life. Eventually, we retreat into our underground bunkers and wait for the war to end, for the waving of the white flag, or the arrival of those two coveted blue lines that say *Pregnant*!

The correct medical term for my Plan B is 'social egg freezing'. Sounds like a party, doesn't it? I mean, it begins with 'social'! The truth is that the egg freezing process is anything but social or fun. When I chose to freeze my eggs, terms like '#MeToo', 'The Women's March', and the women's empowerment movement were not yet embedded in everyday conversation.

As the corporate go-getter, I didn't want to be judged as indulgent because I was choosing to delay having a family until I met the right person. I was part of a wave of women who underwent social egg freezing quietly, with minimal support and without the awareness shared through today's social media. I administered the hormone injections every night, alone.

But this didn't make my shame private.

Picture this: the final egg retrieval can only happen when a trigger injection is administered exactly 24 hours beforehand. You are given a mere 15-minute window for this crucial task. If you do the trigger injection outside of this 15-minute window, the effects on the egg extraction can be catastrophic.

In my case, the moment of truth for this all-important trigger injection coincided with a critical board meeting I simply couldn't skip – though I did try. I even remember thinking, 'How on earth can I change the time of the trigger injection with the IVF clinic?' As always, work took precedence over my personal life, a familiar pattern for me. I could have chosen vulnerability and shared my situation with some trusted colleagues at work, perhaps even explored the possibility of rescheduling the board meeting. But I didn't. I couldn't. It's almost funny how we often let our commitment to work overshadow our personal well-being.

So . . . I was late for the board meeting, and instead of sharing the truth with my fellow directors, I resorted to a feeble excuse and a familiar wave of shame washed over me.

Twenty-four hours later, I groggily blinked my eyes open after the egg retrieval procedure and noticed a small piece of white tape affixed to the back of my hand. On closer inspection, it bore the number '15'. Fifteen eggs had been successfully extracted.

My backup plan was unfolding just as I had hoped. I was firmly back in the driver's seat of my life, able to choose the destination, the speed and even the scenic route along this journey. In giving myself this insurance – that I now had the option of starting a family later in life – I was being brave. Despite the shame that I felt, or the quietness of my actions, there was reassurance in that.

But life doesn't have to be this way – why feel shame at all? Why let it direct our lives, behaviours or decisions? Why did I even consider moving my fertility appointment, just so people at work wouldn't find out?

Changing our relationship with shame

'Shame cannot survive in the presence of love and connection.'

– KAREN A. BAQUIRAN

We have the power to challenge our relationship with shame, to rewrite our own narratives, and to reclaim our voices and our truth. And it all begins with acknowledging that shame is not our master, but merely a temporary obstacle on the path to healing and self-discovery.

> *Shame silences us. Our* Little Brave Acts *help us find our voice.*

They are the declaration that confronts shame, saying, 'You are not helping me, serving me, or allowing me to grow.'

Shame resilience is about welcoming the parts of ourselves that feel the most flawed and vulnerable, while simultaneously holding onto self-love through it all. It's the courage to face the shame that comes with our failures and mistakes, and to offer ourselves compassion in those moments. We all have the strength within us to confront shame, reject it and ultimately rewrite our own narratives, embracing new directions life has in store. Freedom from the shackles of shame can be found on the other side of a *Little Brave Act*.

Through small acts of courage, my clients have also found their own paths towards bravery, moving through the stifling grip of shame. Each of their little steps requires vulnerability, risking rejection, misunderstanding or criticism. Bravery is the raw honesty of sharing with a family member that your marriage is over because you're experiencing domestic violence and you'll be pursuing legal proceedings. It's the courage to disclose your struggles with infertility, daring to ask for support or the privacy and space you need. It's setting up yet another meeting to negotiate a higher pay because you know your worth.

Bravery is all about kneeling down and embracing your screaming toddler, honouring their big messy emotions for as long as it takes, even with all eyes watching you. It's sharing your wins and successes with friends, inviting them to celebrate in a way that's meaningful to you. It's speaking up in the bedroom, articulating your desires to your partner, even if it momentarily disrupts the flow.

Bravery is admitting you don't have plans for New Year's Eve, boldly rejecting the pressure to conform to societal expectations. It's sharing the painful truth that you made decisions in life that led you to not have children, acknowledging the deep anguish it brings while seeking to embrace the new directions your life has taken.

Bravery is recognising that while you fiercely love yourself, you're struggling to love your postpartum body, and that's okay. It's openly acknowledging your intuition and experience of perimenopause, even if science can't yet prove it, and seeking support to navigate this uncharted territory.

When we share our shame, our shame dissolves.

Through such acts of bravery, we can achieve liberation from the suffocating grip of shame. We can reclaim our voices, our truth and our power, forging a path towards healing, growth and self-discovery.

Brave truths

- We don't fear failure. We fear the debilitating feeling of shame when we do fail.

- A brave face is not the same as being brave.

- Shame is the emotion we draw on to ensure we remain safe and hidden.

- Secrets and dishonesty are the hallmarks of shame-based behaviour.

- Quite often there is an intense feeling of freedom on the other side of a brave conversation. Shame silences us. A *Little Brave Act* helps us find our voice.

- *Little Brave Acts* are commonly conversations with those who we fear judgment from the most.

Brave questions

- What parts of your story have you been hiding out of shame, and how can you start to own and share those parts with courage?

- What specific moments or experiences trigger feelings of shame for you, and how can you begin to reframe those moments with compassion?

- How can you practise self-compassion and forgiveness to heal the wounds that shame has created in your life?

- When you feel shame creeping in, what can you do to ground yourself and remind yourself of your worth?

- What would your life look like if you fully let go of shame and embraced your authentic self?

Brave mantra

I release shame by owning my story and practising self-compassion.

CHAPTER 4

The powerful little step of cocooning

'We must let go of the life we have planned, so as to accept the one that is waiting for us. The cave you fear to enter holds the treasure you seek.'

– JOSEPH CAMPBELL

Divorce, redundancy, illness – they can happen in a moment, and there's no instruction manual for what to do next. We can find ourselves in a crumbled heap sobbing on the bathroom floor, wondering what happened to our once-loving marriage; scrolling through job websites at midnight, desperately searching for the security of a pay cheque; or pushing our bodies to heal, puzzled as to how our health could fail us.

Our emotional state becomes erratic – overwhelmed, depressed, anxious and lost. In that moment, using our emotions as a navigational compass may not feel entirely reliable. After our initial plans fail, while we might have a sense of what *not* to do, we don't necessarily have clarity on the right next step.

Welcome to the *liminal space*. The liminal space is that threshold between what was and what is yet to be. As our plans dissolve, we have started to let go of the old version of ourselves, yet the new version has yet to be birthed. We are swinging between two trees, the old vine has been released, but the new one hasn't yet been grasped. Stepping away from your plans, facing failure and confronting shame will feel very disorienting, like stumbling through the dark. We know that growth and transformation can take root in that darkness, but it's hard to let them. It's a time of both exhilarating freedom and daunting uncertainty − and it feels anything but safe.

William Bridges, in *The Way of Transition: Embracing Life's Most Difficult Moments*, emphasises that the liminal space, or what he refers to as the 'neutral zone', is not merely a period of waiting or enduring, but a crucial time for profound inner transformation. He writes, 'It is when we are in transition that we are most completely alive.' This insight underscores the importance of embracing this in-between phase as a fertile ground for growth and renewal, rather than merely a period of uncertainty to be endured.

> *Liminal spaces are the birthplaces of*
> *your next* Little Brave Act.

Once we have entered the liminal space, our next *Little Brave Act* is to allow ourselves to grieve, and to do this we will need to enter a cocoon of healing.

The cocoon of healing

'The soul always knows what to do to heal itself.
The challenge is to silence the mind.'

– CAROLINE MYSS

Cocooning is a profound, transformative period. It's that sacred, tender time when we wrap ourselves up in our own strength and vulnerability, much like a caterpillar spinning a cocoon. We retreat into ourselves, into this intimate space where we can process, heal and reimagine our future. We need time to shed the weight of the past and to embrace the beautiful process of becoming. This is a stage of important introspection and reflection critical to our progress, because otherwise discomfort, messiness and confusion can reign supreme.

When cocooning, we feel like we are losing our way or losing our mind, and most likely our social connections and sense of belonging will become unstable. This is a part of the process. Commonly we fear that if we let go of certain aspects of our lives, we might end up making the wrong choices, and find ourselves at another dead end.

How we handle this time is important. Even with feelings of failure omnipresent, we must confront ourselves to discover hidden aspects of ourselves, perhaps parts of ourselves we never wanted to confront. During this time we live in two worlds – the old one to which we are hanging onto, though it no longer works for us; and the new one we are creating. During this period, time feels confusing – both urgent and suspended.

The oppositional forces of these two worlds often tempt people to leave their cocoons and retreat back to their caterpillar stage, to the perceived security and perhaps excitement of their youth. Others remain stuck in their cocoons for the rest of their lives, afraid of change, afraid of what lies ahead, ignoring the call to transform, unwilling to move forward. Others move in and out of their cocoons, testing to see how far they've come and how far they're yet to go.

Staying in the cocoon

'Just when the caterpillar thought the world was over, it became a butterfly.'

– CHUANG TZU

The cocoon stage is marked by aloneness. This is different from loneliness, which is the aching absence of connection. Aloneness is a deliberate withdrawal into oneself, a quiet space where we shed our old skins. When we are alone, we are able to allow ourselves to feel everything deeply.

I descended into my cocoon stage before I froze my eggs. I was acutely aware that I hadn't met my soulmate yet, and the relentless ticking of my biological clock became an almost physical sensation. There was a deep ache during that period as I mourned the timeline I had once envisioned for myself. I found myself retreating from the noise of the world, seeking solace in solitude. During my cocooning I silently read books that spoke to my soul, I meditated to quiet the chaos in my mind, and I sought the wisdom from those who had walked this path before me. Within this sanctuary, I began to unravel all my tangled emotions: fear, anger, guilt and shame. I moved slowly and deliberately, as my energy waned during this period of time.

In a world of constant connectivity, can we allow ourselves to be alone?

It may not have seemed so at the time, but to remain in the cocoon was an act of bravery. A step towards transformation. I wanted to leave, yet I knew there was still more processing to do. In this space of raw vulnerability, my tears flowed freely and journalling became my lifeline, helping me navigate the storm inside. I felt anger at the unfairness of it all. There was also frustration directed at myself for not having it all figured out, for not being 'where I thought I'd be by now'.

During this time, grief is a demanding and uncooperative friend. I was grieving the loss of precious time, my ability to naturally conceive and my youth. Instead of dance breaks I would take cry breaks. I would let myself sob. Life doesn't stop. But you need to find a way through. I would cry on the way to the gym, grocery shopping, on my morning walk. I could not control when the sadness would engulf me. When I stopped fighting the sadness, it passed through me more quickly. This is the gift of staying within the cocoon.

Processing emotional pain

'You can be shattered and you can put yourself back together, piece by piece, until one day you wake up . . . And no matter how hard you try, you simply cannot fit into your old life anymore. You are like a snake trying to fit into old, dead skin, or a butterfly trying to crawl back into the cocoon.'

– GLENNON DOYLE, *LOVE WARRIOR*

Cocoons can take different shapes and forms. Some cocoons can be ice cold.

I met Leah during a Wim Hof retreat that she was leading. The Wim Hof method uses a combination of ice-cold water exposure, breathing techniques and meditation, where discomfort is embraced as a pathway to strength and resilience. This retreat was for those seeking to enter their cocoon, to transform and then emerge anew.

Between our icy dips Leah shared her raw truth: 'I was separating from my husband and I lost 90 percent of the people in my life overnight. I was in an extreme state of anxiety and depression.'

Transitions can thrust us into loneliness even before cocooning begins, as Leah's story vividly illustrated. Seeking relief, she visited a doctor who offered medication for her anxiety, but in that sterile, clinical space, she heard a voice within her say, 'There is another way.' It was during this time that Leah started to listen to the whispers of her soul. When we are in the cocoon, the silence allows these whispers to be heard.

Her healing journey began with a profound question: 'How can I know myself better?' A podcast featuring Wim Hof's own trials resonated deeply; his journey through loss and resilience struck a chord with Leah. Alone, a single mother drawn to the mountains, she felt called to the process of ice bath immersion.

The morning temperature was nearly freezing. Wrapped up in a woollen beanie and Patagonia thermal jacket, Leah stripped down to her bikini and plunged into the icy Thredbo River for two to three minutes. Like a personal development baptism, she emerged reborn. The next day, she felt the need to do it again. And she couldn't find anyone in her town to do it with her – they all thought she was crazy.

When immersing herself in the icy water, Leah asked herself the question, 'How can I help myself focus on the breath and create distance from the pain I am feeling?' She understood she needed to create distance from the pain in her life to start to see a future with clarity.

Cocooning is the Little Brave Act *of*
stepping back to leap forward.

For 18 months, Leah carved out a cocoon of her own making. Each morning, in a solitary ritual, she ventured to the icy riverbanks with courage and determination. There, in the biting cold, she immersed herself, confronting the deep-seated pain that gripped her body and mind. During this time, she learned about her resilience. She learned to harness the power of her breath, finding strength and calm amidst the chaos in her life.

Leah contemplated her role as a mother and realised that her journey was not just about her own healing. It was about setting an example for her children, teaching them resilience.

She gained clarity around her purpose and grew disciplined, understanding that her new path required resources. She saved diligently, knowing that each dollar would support her in her new direction. Her vision was clear: a life of service, helping others find their strength, just as she had found hers.

'There was this one cold plunge that I did where I merged with my environment,' Leah continued. 'I got a sense of the vastness of my existence. I had not only left my body; I had become the rivers, the trees, and the sense of oneness. I came out of the river and laughed. I realised I was a spiritual being having an experience in my body.'

Having already experienced a cold plunge under Leah's tutelage that morning, I understood what she was referring to. I too had felt that sense of leaving my body.

With this new spiritual insight, she continued, 'After the eighteen months, I went through my divorce with a smile on my face. In fact, I was supporting my husband through the divorce. The cold water helped me learn to cope with stress in a way I never knew possible. The benefit of the plunges is that the cold brings out your biggest fears. If we can do this physically, we then learn how to face our emotional and mental fears in life with extreme resilience.'

Leah's journey, her courage to face the cold, both physically and metaphorically, was a reminder that our cocoons – no matter what form they take – are places of transformation. And emerging from them, we can become something entirely new.

Caroline's powerful little step: leaving the cocoon early

'Every setback is a setup for a comeback. Leaving the cocoon early can feel like a failure, but it's actually an essential part of the process, teaching you what you need to work on when you return to your safe space.'

– MARIANNE WILLIAMSON

The healing process is not entirely linear, nor is it circular. It has no shape. It is chaotic, dramatic, unpredictable and unique to each and every one of us. This means it's okay if sometimes we want to leave the cocoon early, before we are actually ready. We can always re-enter the cocoon later, with more clarity of why we are there.

After walking away from her marriage, Caroline prioritised healing and self-discovery in her cocoon. In it, she surrendered and let go of the life she was living in order to access a closer connection to who she really was, learning about how her childhood past affected her present, even though at times it left her feeling disorientated.

Caroline herself left her cocoon early.

'There are so many cute guys out there to date,' Caroline's best friend told her. 'You will love it. You just need to get out there and give it a go.'

We all have that friend, who may be at a different stage of their own healing journey. They encourage us to join them, sometimes when we are not quite ready.

Caroline decided to leave her cocoon temporarily – to reset, to reassess and recognise how far she had come, but also to see how far she still needed to go.

Her first little step was setting up an online dating profile, 18 months after leaving her marriage, and starting to swipe left and right. She was allowing herself to contemplate intimacy, romance and the possibility of creating a hybrid family. But was Caroline ready?

'I started to notice who I was attracting and how I felt. To be honest, I was not really attracting anyone special, or anyone that excited me. I met someone and we had a brief fling. It was interesting because it brought up all my fears of being a single mum. He asked during our date, "How are you going to find time to date when you're a mum to four kids?" I was devastated. He had said out loud my greatest fear.'

When we leave the safety of the cocoon, a womb where we feel protected and try and rebirth ourselves, we are back out in the wilderness of our life. Sometimes we need life to reflect uncomfortable truths. No longer able to deflect pain to her ex-husband, Caroline needed to face the uncomfortable truth of where she was and where she wanted to be.

'After that, I started to avoid telling people my personal story. And then I realised, I come as a package, me and my boys, and you accept me for who I am. I realised I hadn't really fully healed a lot of those wounds that I still had when I went out there to date. It was almost like a bit of a test for my healing.'

Leaving the cocoon temporarily can be important
for our healing journey to accelerate.

Within days, Caroline removed herself from the dating apps and re-entered her cocoon with greater intention, vigour and clarity about how this cocoon stage was helping her. For years she committed to personal transformation work. She even erected a yurt on her property for a women's circle on the weekend, which was like a cocoon.

When we enter our own cocoons and transform, we begin to support others around us to do this work. Her yurt was a safe place where these women could enter and experience the beginning of another revolution of their own healing work. Caroline knew that this would be uncomfortable, revealing and healing. But she was now equipped to support them.

Cocooning with others

'Women instinctually know how to nourish each other, and just being with each other is healing.'

– TANJA TAALJARD

Sometimes, there's this magnetic pull, a deep gut feeling, to retreat and cocoon ourselves from the world with other women. When my friend Lisa invited me to a womb retreat, I instantly said yes, even though I had no clue what I was diving into. When we cocoon with masters and teachers who have walked further than we have, with a deep well of wisdom to tap into, magic happens. After we all arrived, the circle began, and as we shared our stories, I realised each woman was there with her own blend of pain and hope. Some were grappling with the relentless agony of endometriosis; others were lost in the confusing maze of unexplained infertility. There were those enduring the silent suffering of painful periods, and a few who just needed to escape their marriages for a while. I was still hoping to one day become a mother, craving a space where I could be with women who truly understood. We could share our struggles and feel profoundly heard and seen.

When we step into the cocoon of a retreat, we might not always know what we're searching for. But upon reflection, it becomes clear that we were all there seeking the same thing – a rebirth, a chance to reclaim our relationship with our bodies and our feminine power. We weren't just healing our wounds; we were reconnecting with the deepest parts of ourselves, finding our way back to wholeness.

Can you give yourself permission to go to a retreat to cocoon?

In one unforgettable moment, we gathered around a woman lying on a white bedsheet. We wrapped her in it, like a cocoon, encasing her in a sacred womb of love and support. As I watched this ritual unfold, tears streamed down my face, each drop a testament to the pain I had carried for so long. I cried for all the times I had let men take advantage of me, for the moments I had swallowed my 'no' and stayed when I wanted to leave. I cried for the women in my ancestral line who were silenced, who couldn't find their voices, who stayed when they longed to break free. I hadn't realised my womb carried so much grief, the energy of unwanted memories and the sadness of self-betrayal. Healing doesn't mean the damage never existed. It means the damage no longer controls our lives. This process was a rebirth, a release of emotions that no longer served us.

I came to understand that this cocooning was not just for myself – it was for all of us. It was about the intergenerational healing that had long been awaiting its time. When we cocoon, we are not merely doing it for ourselves. We are doing it for our mothers, our grandmothers and all the women who came before us, who could not find the space or voice to do it themselves. In this sacred act, we are transforming their pain into our power, reclaiming our bodies, our stories, our very essence. We are breaking ancient cycles: one tear, one cocoon, one rebirth at a time. In that profound moment, surrounded by these courageous women, I realised that cocooning is not meant to be done in isolation but in the collective embrace of other women. When we heal together, the healing is magnified, as we bear witness to the pain within ourselves and each other, releasing what no longer serves us.

Our womb carries not only our stories but also the echoes of our ancestors' pain and joy.

After this profound experience, we sat silently over lunch, sipping a vegetable soup that felt like a balm for the soul. Surrounded by these women who had been cracked open, we were able to sit in silence with ourselves and each other. This is the gift of cocooning on a retreat. After lunch, some of us took to our journals, while others paired off to share their stories. We were listening for ourselves in each other's stories, or reflecting internally in the deep, nourishing silence the retreat offered.

The words you speak to your womb can transform your life. Let them be words of love, healing and empowerment.

I left the retreat with three big realisations. First off, I am not a failure for embarking on this IVF journey. Going through IVF doesn't make me less of a woman; in the cocoon of the retreat, I discovered the warrior within me fighting for what I deeply desired. Second, my womb hasn't let me down. No, the truth is, I haven't been listening to her. She's been trying to tell me her story, her needs, her pains, and I've been too busy, too distracted to truly hear her. Lastly, the power of sisterhood and shared stories is nothing short of transformative. When women come together and share their truths, something magical happens.

We find strength in each other's stories, we heal together, and we realise that we are not alone. The gifts of cocooning with others is immeasurable.

Breaking free

They say a butterfly must beat its wings hard against the shell of the cocoon in order to break free. This resonates with me, because of course it's hard to leave and start a new life. I had many difficult days while cocooned, and would beat my wings though they weren't yet fully formed or ready for full flight. Leaving the cocoon in these times was only temporary and I would need to return to further heal.

Looking back, I could have benefitted from more cocooning after many of my relationship break-ups, as I would too quickly find myself in another relationship with similar problems. By not giving myself a chance to fully recover from the pain of the last break-up, to really think about that relationship and how it had and hadn't serviced my needs and wants, I kept making similar mistakes.

Even very intense situations don't have to leave psychological scars, if we are willing to process our changes at a deeper level. Back then, I still had to learn the process of taking *Little Brave Acts* to stay in the cocoon and do the work.

I had to understand that true healing requires time, introspection and the bravery to face our own truths. It's in that sacred space of the cocoon where we unravel, reflect and ultimately transform. Only then can we emerge stronger, wiser, and ready to break the patterns that no longer serve us.

Brave truths

- It is a *Little Brave Act* to enter a cocoon to allow ourselves to grieve, heal and process our emotional pain.

- The cocoon stage is marked by aloneness. This is different from loneliness, which is the aching absence of connection. Aloneness is the space to connect to ourselves.

- We need to stay in the cocoon to allow our full transformation to happen.

- You may feel called to leave your cocoon early. That is okay. You will return more committed to the process of transformation.

- Cocooning with other women is powerful and will amplify and accelerate your healing.

Brave questions

- Do you need to enter a cocoon to heal? Are you resisting entering your cocoon? If so, why?

- What pain are you holding onto that needs to be released?

- What tools, resources, mentors or coaches can help you process your emotional pain right now?

- How do you practise self-compassion in your cocoon?

- What new strengths or insights are emerging from your cocoon?

Brave mantra

I honour this time of cocooning. I embrace being alone and healing.

CHAPTER 5

The powerful little step of letting go of plans

'If Plan A didn't work, the alphabet has 25 more letters'

– UNKNOWN

When our Plan A fails, we can quickly scramble for a backup – a plan borne out of a crisis, or a necessity, just as I did when I froze my eggs. We feel unsure about the road ahead because we are still clinging to our initial plan, the one we poured our hopes and dreams into. We may find ourselves constantly looking over our shoulder at the past, consumed by a mindset of regret. We second-guess ourselves with those unhelpful 'what if' questions. 'What if I had worked harder? Tried harder? Hadn't given up? Would my Plan A have eventually succeeded?' These questions haunt us, keeping us tethered to a vision that no longer serves us.

Plan B

We don't want to stray too far from our original Plan A, so we come up with a *compromised plan,* Plan B. We're stuck in a loop of self-doubt, unable to fully embrace the new path that might be calling us. We settle for something that's safer, easier, less scary. But here's the thing: Plan B is often just Plan A in disguise, and it lacks the fire, the passion, and the honesty that comes from truly listening to our hearts and being brave enough to follow what we hear.

The positive reframe is that even when we compromise, it's a step towards growth. Plan B may not be perfect, but it's still progress in the right direction.

The truth is that we are part way through our healing journey. We have started making changes in our lives, but not enough to rock our comfortable boats. We are diving into the waters of transformation; however, there is still a depth beneath for us to swim.

We have also been fed a fairytale lie that once we leave the safety of the cocoon the butterfly spreads her wings and flies off to marry a prince and have his babies. We're told that after our first failure, we'll bounce back up, dust ourselves off, and keep going without a hitch – never having to worry about failing again. We believe we'll continue to make progress and rise beyond our setbacks with ease. Yet in reality, we may need to cocoon not once, but many times. After going through a challenging divorce, you may find yourself facing unexpected legal battles over custody. Having navigated the emotional turmoil of fertility treatments, you may finally conceive, only to encounter high-risk pregnancy complications. As a single parent, you may have adjusted to the new dynamics and routines, only to find that, suddenly your child faces significant academic challenges that demand your full attention.

These are the real stories, the ones we don't often talk about, but need to. Because this is life – unpredictable and imperfect.

Many years ago, I lost my job, and I knew deep down it was time to start my spiritual business. I was terrified of judgment and uncertain about this career move. So instead of stepping into the *Little Brave Act* of pursuing this new path, I resorted to Plan B: finding a part-time finance manager role. I went to interview after interview, facing constant rejections. When I finally landed a job, my Plan B had technically worked. But from the very first day, I hated it.

I had compromised. I had deceived myself, evading true bravery. This is what many Plan Bs look like – a consolation prize, a runner-up trophy, second place. They're the safer paths chosen out of fear of pursuing our true purpose. That's why they often falter, and quickly. Because they lack the passion, the authenticity, and the wholehearted commitment that comes from following our true path.

Plan B may be Plan A in fancy dress.

Stepping into *any* Plan B invites a repetition of disappointment. Plan B might seem like a safety net, but it often traps us in mediocrity and dissatisfaction. It's like trying to convince ourselves that settling is the same as thriving. But deep down, we know it's not. We know we're capable of more, deserving of more.

When Plan B fails

'Just because you made a good plan, doesn't mean that's what's gonna happen.'

– TAYLOR SWIFT

When my husband Tyson and I were presented with the opportunity to be part of a new and exploratory IVF documentary, one that would span two and a half years of filming (although we didn't know that at the time), it took a little bit of bravery and a lot of courage to say 'yes'. Alongside other couples, Tyson and I were to reveal all the highs, lows and monotony of what can be a deeply private, desperate and confronting journey. I mean, who wouldn't want to be filmed while weeing on a pregnancy stick or lying on your back, legs propped up in stirrups? I do like a challenge.

Some challenges test your limits, while others threaten to break you. Would this challenge be the one to break me? What my husband and I did not know at the time, is that we would be embarking on one of the most challenging times of our life.

I didn't break, but I got close.

It's a profoundly long and solemn minute, the wait for the results of a pregnancy test. Those 15 eggs, carefully preserved when I was a sprightly 38-year-old, were my lifeline. Eleven entered the thawing process, seven joined forces with my husband's sperm, four dared to grow. And after five days of anticipation, only one emerged as a 'viable embryo'. I gasped when I found this out. From 15 possible chances, we actually ended up with only one attempt.

They say one embryo is all it takes, and I clung to that hope – my miracle embryo.

Adding to my hope was the x-factor that the embryo was at least made from much younger eggs. The statistics for conceiving a child using my own eggs at the age of 45 through IVF were breathtakingly low, only a 1 to 2 percent chance. I was, after all, at that stage in life where friends around me were starting to display perimenopausal symptoms while raising their teenage children. But not me. I had successfully turned back my biological clock. With the help of my younger eggs, my odds had substantially improved, reaching nearly 30 percent. IVF was bound to work – my daily mantra.

Not only that, but my breasts felt full and swollen, my belly round, no monthly period had arrived. So, I sat there on the toilet with cameras rolling, pregnancy test in hand, and a sense of certainty. You see, when you make a plan and execute it with bravery, things unfold just as you hope they will. Don't they? I *knew* that I was pregnant.

I stared with confidence into the camera and what would be millions of faces in 12 months' time – the faces of women who had struggled for years to conceive, or who were still struggling, women who had grown-up kids and conceived through IVF, parents who never could conceive, and those with big happy families wondering how they got so lucky – I wanted them all to know there was hope; and with a positive pregnancy test result, I could. I gave a quiet confident smile and discreetly pulled up my underwear.

Waiting the full minute for those two blue lines to appear felt like an eternity, but finally the results flashed in Vegas neon lights on the pregnancy test: *not* pregnant.

My legs weakened, a distant ringing filled my ears, and my heart raced as if searching for an escape. A desperate, anguished scream escaped from the depths of my throat that became a crying wail of 'Oh no!'

Amidst uncontrollable sobs, my husband held me close, while I repeated 'I am sorry' over and over. It wasn't just my own longing to become a mother; he, too, harboured the deep desire to embrace fatherhood. He too had invested in my Plan B. I was angry, shocked and numb. There was a range of emotions I could not label or comprehend in that moment.

My cherished Plan B had failed.

The rest of the day dragged on with excruciating slowness, each second feeling like an eternity. I let phone calls go unanswered, as no one could find the right words to offer comfort. We were too exhausted to process the next step of the journey we needed to go on together. We needed time to come to terms with the failure of our Plan B.

But with time running out, we also needed to immediately start trying IVF with *my* eggs at the age of 45. We couldn't waste even a single precious monthly cycle. There was no time to grieve or reflect. Daily injections became a painful routine, accompanied by early morning blood tests that felt like a relentless intrusion into our already disrupted lives. Cycle after cycle seemed to end in disappointment, each failed attempt chipping away at our hopes and resilience. My Plan B *wasn't* working.

Weekends away became less about relaxation and more about navigating the logistical challenges of fertility treatments.

Our once vibrant optimism slowly gave way to a sense of quiet desperation. By now we were on our seventh heart-wrenching IVF cycle using my own eggs. Could I dare to believe in miracles anymore, when the reality was a whopping 98 percent chance of failure? It's the kind of statistic that makes you question whether optimism is a brave stance or just a form of denial. We even had the latest fertilised embryo undergo testing for abnormalities. The verdict? Two chromosomal defects, sealing the fate of its viability. It would not have implanted successfully.

Yet amidst the chaos and uncertainty, we persevered, clinging to the flickering flame of hope that someday, one day, our efforts would be rewarded with the miracle we so desperately longed to receive.

I had to surrender to the process.

When we are experiencing multiple failures over a prolonged period of time, we can tell ourselves all the wise, empowering things about how failure is a stepping stone, how it builds character, how it's part of the journey. But in those raw moments when our hearts are broken repeatedly, our dreams feel shattered and we're left questioning our worth, it's painful.

Experiencing multiple failures is a visceral experience that shakes us to our core. It makes us doubt ourselves, our choices, our path. We feel the sting of rejection, the weight of disappointment, the ache of unmet expectations. And it's okay to acknowledge that. It's okay to sit with that pain, to feel it deeply.

During this time, my *Little Brave Acts* included simply showing up for my blood tests while fighting back feelings of despair. Or gritting my teeth determined, as I injected hormones into my bruised stomach. Or lacing up my sneakers and hitting the pavement with a heavy sad heart, knowing that I had to move my body. Or putting on my game face and showing up for my business and clients, serving their needs. I knew I had to stay brave, as my Plan B was starting to show cracks too.

During this time, I was learning to take off my superhero cape and extend great compassion to myself. I found the anger, guilt and resentment at the process started to dissolve. This is the essence of healing.

When life doesn't go according to plan

'Do not judge me by my successes, judge me by how many times I fell down and got back up again. Plan B might fail due to reasons beyond your control, but your resilience is what truly matters.'

– NELSON MANDELA

Sometimes Plan B might not work out, and it's not because you did anything wrong. It's just part of the journey. Many of my clients reach out to work with me when they're in the eye of their storm. Erica walked into my office looking for a mediumship reading. She wanted to connect with her late husband. It was his birthday, and fate had granted her a free appointment today. I was thrilled by the synchronicity. In that first session, I discovered Rob's love for sausage sandwiches, on white bread, drowned in tomato sauce and his passion for motorbikes. He was a gentle giant with a wicked sense of humour.

She told me, 'I remember our first date like it was yesterday. He was six foot seven, in brown work shorts and boots, with scruffy hair. He didn't drink alcohol – just hot tea. I wanted to run, thinking this is never going to work. It wasn't love at first sight. But slowly, a deep, unbreakable bond formed – we would laugh until we cried.'

'Our world turned upside down the day Rob was diagnosed with ALS. Rob, true to his character, faced the doctor and said, 'Well, we all have to die sometime,' Erica revealed. 'We would sit on the veranda for hours, under the stars, pouring out our hearts about death, sharing our fearless belief in the afterlife. One year later, he was gone, and my life was forever altered.'

We don't know how brave we are until being brave is our only choice. Erica's life plunged into the paradox of trying to live when a part of her had died.

Erica shared much more than just her grief. 'My first marriage ended suddenly in my 20s; and my second marriage was emotionally and physically abusive in my 30s. When I met Rob in my 40s, I thought, 'This is my third chance at a wonderful life, especially in the later years.' We bought a big, beautiful apartment on the Gold Coast. The balcony was massive. Rob loved to dance, and we'd talk about one day dancing on that balcony as the sun set.'

Erica was learning the lesson of surrender and letting go. It was time for her to cocoon, free from distractions that stymie healing. Her hope to be married and settled in her 30s ended painfully – her Plan A.

Meeting Rob was her next plan, her Plan B, and it brought her immense joy. But life has a way of teaching us not to cling to any plans.

A year later, Erica knocked on my door. 'I'm back. It's Rob's birthday again.' We spent an hour laughing and crying, reconnecting with Rob. She was learning to walk forward a little taller, carrying the weight of grief a little lighter. Yet her life was still in the chaotic flux that hits when death knocks on our door.

'I am so lost. I just don't know what to do.' Her eyes filled with tears. 'It hurts so much. How do I keep going? I keep wondering, why am I left behind? Why him and not me?'

I looked her in the eye and said, 'Erica, you are in the midst of the hardest part. You're in the cocoon, and it's messy and dark in there. But this is where transformation happens. You're not lost – you're growing and evolving.'

It was time for her to dive deep into healing, to tap into her spiritual abilities. Her intuition and heart screamed, 'Yes!', even though her mind resisted. Erica's journey wasn't about finding a new plan. Erica's *Little Brave Act* was about letting go, accepting that when life doesn't go according to plan, it presents an opportunity to learn how to live fully in the absence of certainty.

Finding strength in letting go of plans

'You never know how strong you are until being strong is your only choice.'

– BOB MARLEY

I was mindlessly scrolling through TikTok – down a black hole of cat memes, cooking fail videos, and clips of people attempting the latest dance crazes – when this one video came up that I watched five times in a row, mesmerised, my thumb suspended in air.

It was a story of bravery, a tale that unfolded on one of the most visible days for a woman: her wedding day. For most brides, it's a day filled with anticipation and joy, where they shine in the spotlight of love and celebration. Not for Kayley Stead. She found herself facing a darkness she never could have imagined. Kayley got a curveball the size of Everest on the morning of her big day, when the groom's father called her to let her know that her partner of almost four years would not be coming to the wedding.

Now, in the realm of wedding day nightmares, this ranks up there with accidentally setting the dress on fire. But did Kayley crumble? Oh, no! She grabbed bravery by the bouquet and waltzed through her day like a boss.

For most brides, the thought of walking down the aisle and not finding their partner waiting for them is unfathomable, a nightmare scenario they would never even consider. And a groom not turning up would most likely bring a level of shame incomprehensible for most brides.

But Kayley didn't let being left at the altar define her – she refused to let her groom's betrayal overshadow the celebration of love and unity and, with unwavering resolve, she did everything pretty much as she had meticulously planned, from her grand wedding entrance to the sumptuous meal, heartfelt speeches and joyous dances. In a breathtaking display of strength and resilience, Kayley posed for professional photos alone. As she walked through the sparkler tunnel at the end of the night, a path illuminated by the love and support of her family and friends, she did so with grace and dignity. The TikTok video showed a woman embracing each wedding tradition as a *Little Brave Act*.

In each of those moments, she could have fallen into a heap; yet she met each moment with grace. What was so impressive about Kayley was that, even without a groom, she shone at the centre of her wedding day *and* she shared that with the world to inspire others. There was no shame present.

Now, Kayley was not the first woman to be left at the altar, nor will she be the last. But what set Kayley apart was not just her heartbreak, but how she navigated through it with an unparalleled level of bravery and resilience.

In fact, her story resonated so deeply with people all around the world that her TikTok video reached viral status, her story was then picked up by most of the major media outlets, and thus every *Little Brave Act* she stepped into throughout her solo wedding day propelled her onto the world stage.

As I watched the reel on repeat, I found myself engulfed in a whirlwind of emotions, each frame of Kayley's story stirring a reflection of my own wedding day, months before. The thought that Tyson might have failed to show up sent shivers down my spine, plunging me into a realm of hypothetical scenarios that I struggled to comprehend.

Could I have mustered the strength to smile through tears as I posed for photos alone, my heart and my spirit broken? Could I have forced myself to partake in the wedding meal, every morsel of food a bitter reminder of the betrayal? Could I have summoned the courage to dance, fearing that my legs might give way beneath me under the weight of heartbreak? Could I have found the words to deliver a speech, my voice cracking with emotion as I grappled with the disbelief of my position?

The truth is, the mere thought of facing such a scenario would probably have filled me with a paralysing sense of shame. The weight of expectation, the burden of societal norms, the fear of judgment. Worst of all, I would have had to bear not just my own shame, but that of my mother and father, whose dreams for my wedding day would have been shattered alongside mine. Their pitying glances, their whispered words of sympathy – they would have served as constant reminders of the pain I carried, a burden I would have been forced to shoulder for the rest of my days. I'm glad that was one failed plan I didn't have to face!

Frankly, the way Kayley coped was nothing short of extraordinary. Not only did she let go of her initial plan, but she immediately embraced an entirely new plan. In the face of devastating betrayal, she chose not to retreat into the shadows of shame and despair, but to stand tall and face her pain head-on. Her courage in the midst of heartbreak struck a chord with millions, serving as a beacon of hope for anyone struggling to deal with shame in their darkest moments, and inspiring others to trust that failed plans simply herald new plans, different plans. Better plans.

What I learned most from watching Kayley's video go viral was that we all *want* to be as strong as she was that day. We really do. We share the clip, telling each other: *this* is how you cope when a situation drags you down into the worst shame spiral you could ever imagine.

Kayley's message was powerful for three main reasons.

Firstly, she normalised plans failing, telling the world, 'This bad thing happened to me and I did survive.'

Secondly, she demonstrated the power of rallying her community around her to get her through that tough 24-hour period and beyond. When we share our shame our shame dissolves.

Thirdly, she didn't catastrophise the situation, even though her failed plan *was* the epitome of a catastrophe. She broke the whole situation down into small challenges and met each one with her own unique *Little Brave Act*.

While we may not think that we have that kind of bravery, I don't think Kayley thought she did either, until she found herself in that situation. Potentially, the biggest takeaway for us all is that, if we were to be thrown into the bowels of such chaos, we too could respond in the same way. We just need to back ourselves and realise that we may need to take our own little steps towards bravery in the way that Kayley did. She has now voiced her story on many self-help podcasts and taken the next little step by re-entering the dating scene, ready to open her heart again to love.

Leaning into multiple failures

'I've missed more than 9,000 shots in my career. I've lost almost 300 games. 26 times I've been trusted to take the game-winning shot and missed. I've failed over and over and over again in my life. And that is why I succeed.'

– MICHAEL JORDAN

I remember when Tyson and I were strolling down the red carpet for the launch of the television documentary, *Big Miracles*, my first-ever red-carpet experience. On the outside, I was attempting to exude positivity and enthusiasm. But on the inside, I was devastated.

The launch party was to be a gathering of all the heroic IVF doctors, empathic nurses and supportive admin staff involved in the show, all eager to watch the first episode of *Big Miracles*. But this wasn't just any premiere – it was a moment poised to change the landscape of television history. Other reality television shows had delved into issues dealing with personal growth, self-discovery and positive transformation. Programs such as *Dating on the Spectrum* and *Alone* had tackled some particularly deep and meaningful topics. But *Big Miracles* was to tackle the one taboo subject that remained largely untouched: the journey of IVF. I was, in truth, thrilled to be a part of the experience.

Tyson and I found ourselves among strangers yet bound by a shared journey marked by hope and heartache. With open hearts, we tentatively asked the show's producers at the launch, 'Have the others found success?'

They diplomatically honoured the privacy of the other couples' journeys, potentially shielding our fragile hearts from the overwhelming joy of others having a newborn.

But then, a couple entered, clearly nestled in a beautiful bubble of joy – their new baby sleeping in a carrier.

A lump swelled in my throat and my breath quickened. 'They did it,' I murmured to Tyson, who squeezed my hand in silent solidarity. In that tender moment, we shared an understanding that sometimes words fall short in the face of profound disappointment.

But then another couple entered, cradling their precious bundle of joy; then another couple with their baby, and another with theirs. And as the crowd gathered around the glowing mothers, we couldn't help but feel a bittersweet ache, a poignant reminder of the miracle that had thus far eluded us.

Finally, as the final credits rolled on the first episode, there was an unexplainable atmosphere in the room. With every frame, every spoken word, we were reshaping the conversation in households across Australia about IVF and fertility challenges. We were giving a face, a voice and a narrative to the experiences of the one-in-three-women who endure these challenges silently, stoically and painfully.

But amidst all the buzz and celebration, I turned to my husband, my heart heavy with the weight of unspoken fears. I finally managed to choke out the words, 'Were we the only ones who didn't succeed?'

He hesitated for a moment before gently confirming, 'Yes, I think so, darling.'

And in that moment, tears streamed down my face, unstoppable and raw. 'Oh my God,' I gasped, the weight of our unfulfilled hopes crashing down around us.

As the reality sank in, my mind raced with a single thought: Australia is about to witness my IVF journey end in failure. This is going to be excruciating. I'm the only one who didn't make it.

Suddenly, the prospect of being showcased on national television transformed from a hopeful opportunity into what felt like the pinnacle of tragedy.

The weight of that realisation brought forth a wave of debilitating anxiety that would shadow me for the next six weeks as the television show aired. Each episode, each moment captured on screen, felt like a painful reminder of my multiple failures.

Stepping off the red carpet felt less like a glamorous exit and more like standing on the shores of the Red Sea – only this time there was no miraculous parting of the waves or crowd, just an overwhelming flood of emotions drowning me, emotions shared by countless women navigating the tumultuous waters of fertility struggles.

You might think I was brave for putting myself out there on national television, but the truth is, when the universe first whispered in our ears and we said 'yes' to being filmed, it was just an exploratory documentary, not yet picked up by a major network. We believed in the project, in its message, in the passion and dedication of everyone involved. And, perhaps naively, we also believed in our Plan B – in our own journey succeeding. In hindsight, saying 'yes' was a small act of bravery, a leap of faith into the unknown. Now I would need more bravery than ever before to continue. My vision was strong, my heart was hopeful, my mind was uncertain.

Ryan Holiday, in *The Obstacle is the Way*, teaches us that repeated failures and obstacles are not barriers, but pathways to success. He writes, 'The obstacle in the path becomes the path. Never forget, within every obstacle is an opportunity to improve our condition.' This philosophy became my guiding light, reminding me that each failure was a stepping stone, not a dead end.

After each episode aired, I purposefully engaged in deep rest, shed tears and nurtured myself – these were all *Little Brave Acts* I had to muster during that challenging time. And leaning into the loving embrace of my husband each night, allowing myself to feel the weight of my emotions, was yet another small act of courage.

Sometimes facing the failure of your Plan B can feel harder than facing the failure of your Plan A. But once we let go of those plans, we can fully embrace the transformational work required to heal and move forward.

Brave truths

- When our Plan A fails, we may scramble to a backup plan - our Plan B. This is quite often a compromised plan.

- It is important to learn to let go of our Plan A and B and not look backward, but forward.

- Our Plan B will still feel linked to parts of our old life that no longer serve us.

- We come to know our true strength in enduring multiple failures of both Plan A and Plan B.

- Failing of our Plan B asks us to dive deeper into our inner healing work.

Brave questions

- What truth about your life are you resisting right now? What is this failure trying to teach you about your path forward?

- In what ways are you still holding onto old stories or beliefs that no longer serve you?

- How can you redefine success for yourself, beyond traditional plans and expectations?

- What fears are surfacing now that your plans have failed? How can you face these fears with compassion?

- What would it look like to trust yourself completely in this moment of uncertainty?

Brave mantra

I surrender to the life that is waiting for me.

PART 3
Transforming

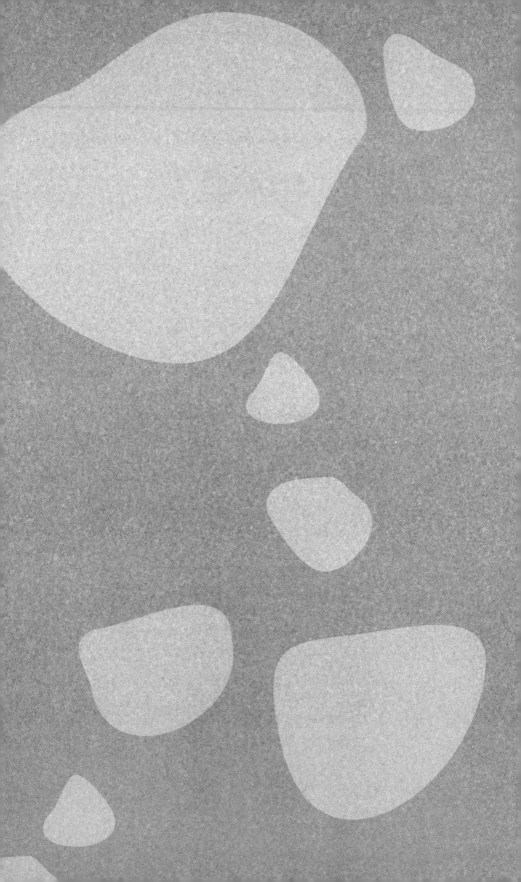

CHAPTER 6

The powerful little step of visioning

'The only thing worse than being blind is having sight but no vision.'

– HELEN KELLER

Having a clear vision of the life we want isn't just about setting goals; it's about infusing our lives with purpose and direction. This vision often gets sidelined when we're busy creating our Plan A and Plan B, trying to fit into moulds that were never made for us. But it's time to bring it back to the forefront. When we let go of our fixed plans, we need to find a bold vision for ourselves – one where we dream big and unapologetically. Our *Little Brave Acts*, those little steps we take every day, become so much more potent when they're aligned with a vision that truly resonates with our hearts.

Your vision is the blueprint for your dreams.

Sometimes our Plan A fails because our vision wasn't as expansive as it needed to be – we were playing it small, tiptoeing around the edges of our comfort zone, thinking we're living boldly when, in reality, we're still trapped within boundaries of familiarity.

A lot of the coaching I do is to help women step into the life of their dreams and break free from their lacklustre status quo. In the process of helping them create a vision for their life, I ask a lot of questions about what they value, what work they would do if time and money was not an issue, what true joy and relaxation looks like. These might sound like easy questions to answer; but, interestingly, they are often met with hesitant nods, vacant stares or resistance. Why?

These questions involve the little step of putting ourselves first and the *Little Brave Act* of prioritising our needs. Society tells us that we are supposed to be perfect mothers, perfect wives, perfect employees. We have been conditioned to believe that our worth is tied to how well we conform to these impossible standards. So, when it comes to creating a vision for our lives, we're paralysed by fear – fear of judgment, of failure, of not measuring up. And let's not forget the guilt – the guilt of wanting something more, of daring to put our own needs and desires first for once.

Three issues I commonly see with vision setting are: the false vision, no vision or a small vision.

False visions

False visions are those crafted by society, by our families, by others who seek to shape us into their image of who we should be. They are the cookie-cutter dreams handed down to us by well-meaning parents, by cultural expectations, by social media. They tell us that success hinges on external markers: wealth, status, accolades. Despite knowing deep down that true fulfilment goes beyond material possessions, we are often seduced into basing our vision on inauthentic promises, leading us into a state of delusion.

These false visions often rely on dependence, suggesting that success hinges on something or someone else – perhaps a man's provision, or unwavering loyalty leading to eventual promotion. Such false visions perpetuate the myth, for example, that pregnancy is solely determined by effort, ignoring the complexities of fertility, or that we become invisible after 50, barren and bereft of vitality.

With my own eggs frozen and stored, I had a false vision of my own. I presumed that, with my 38-year-old eggs preserved, any future IVF success was bound to be successful, and my loved ones would commend me for my astute forethought. Little did I know how dependent this vision was on other factors beyond just having younger eggs.

Commonly rooted in seeking external approval, such false visions foster a mindset of passivity, rather than empowering us to take control of our own lives right now.

As a coach for women, I've seen firsthand the harm these false visions can cause. In my sessions, I guide women towards financial independence, empowerment in all aspects of their fertility journey, and seizing opportunities in their careers – without waiting for validation from others.

Breaking free from our false visions is not easy, yet it is the essential work needed to create a new foundation for our life. The first step is to be able to see that the vision is false, that it is not serving our authentic selves.

No vision

Then there is the issue of having no vision. Living without our own vision is like being caught in a never-ending whirlwind of busyness, drowning in the demands of everyday life, and feeling utterly drained. It's a cycle that keeps us stuck, going nowhere fast. Creating a vision for ourselves can feel like just another daunting task on our never-ending to-do list. It's not urgent, so it often gets relegated to the bottom and never checked off.

But here's the thing: when we lack our own vision, we inadvertently become servants to other people's visions instead. At first, it may feel fulfilling to contribute to someone else's life purpose; but deep down, we know we're betraying ourselves. We sacrifice our dreams for the sake of others – staying late at work to finish a report instead of pursuing our side hustle or declining a girls' trip to maintain the family routine at home. We suppress our desires, burying them beneath a façade of composure and dependability. Eventually, the pressure builds, and like a dormant volcano we reach a breaking point, erupting with pent-up anger and resentment at the injustice of it all.

Small visions

The third common issue relates to playing small. Settling for a small vision might seem safe and comfortable, but it's limiting, stifling and ultimately unfulfilling. Why do we accept a small vision when we know we are capable of a much larger one? In his book *The Big Leap*, Gay Hendricks delves into the concept of the 'upper limit problem'. He suggests that early in life we develop a happiness threshold. When we start to experience success or we get close to the realisation of a dream, then unworthiness or guilt creeps in and we limit the joy we are meant to experience.

Hendricks explains that when we reach our perceived upper limit of success, abundance, or love, we subconsciously sabotage ourselves, fearing we've ventured too far beyond what we believe we deserve. Over time, this self-sabotage causes our vision for ourselves to shrink, limiting our potential and preventing us from fully embracing the abundance that life has to offer. It's a cycle that keeps us trapped in mediocrity unless we consciously break free from these limiting beliefs and expand our vision for what's possible.

Michael Hyatt, in *The Vision Driven Leader*, highlights the transformative power of visionary thinking. He writes, 'Vision is the indispensable factor that propels us to achieve dreams we once thought impossible. A compelling vision inspires us to break through barriers and realise our full potential.' This insight emphasises that by embracing a visionary mindset, we can break free from limitations and design a life that truly reflects our deepest aspirations and values.

The benefits of a vision

When I coach women to have their own vision and to step into this vision, there are two main benefits that open for them.

Firstly, when you have your own sense of purpose and direction in life, it becomes much easier to nurture your self-esteem and to let go of envy. Why? Because you're no longer comparing yourself to others or measuring your success based on external markers. Instead, you're focused on your own journey, your own growth, and your own unique path. You understand that everyone's journey is different, and that there's no point in comparing yourself to others. Your vision gives you a sense of fulfilment and satisfaction that can't be shaken by someone else's success. You're too busy chasing your own dreams to worry about what other people are doing. In the end, having your own vision is the antidote to low self-esteem and to envy – it frees you from the need for validation from others.

Stress is an unavoidable part of modern life. However, not all stress is detrimental. When you have your own vision it puts you in charge of the kind of stress that you experience in your life. This is where the concept of *eustress* versus *distress* comes into play.

Eustress is the positive kind of stress – the kind that comes from pursuing meaningful goals and stretching yourself outside your comfort zone, such as running a marathon or starting a podcast. It's the adrenaline rush you feel when you're tackling a new challenge or pushing yourself to new heights. It is often described as the stress 'on the way' to your goals. And yes, you will experience challenges when pursuing your vision.

Distress, on the other hand, is the negative kind of stress, the kind that comes from feeling overwhelmed, out of control, or stuck in a situation that feels hopeless, such as the dead-end job or the relationship that is more of a situationship. This is the kind of stress that we experience when we lack our own vision. It can be described as the stress 'in the way' of your goals.

When you have your own vision, you're more likely to experience eustress than distress, positive stress not negative stress, because you're actively engaged in creating the life you want. Choosing your vision means you are in the driver's seat of choosing your stress - and this is empowering.

The power of your vision

'What you stay focused on will grow.'
–Roy T. Bennett

While our plans may dissolve, we must hold tight to our vision. Plans can shift, fall apart or take unexpected turns. But our vision – our heart's true north – must remain steady. Our vision is like a GPS that keeps rerouting when we miss a turn or, you know, when we decide to stop for donuts.

I've quietly defied the odds in so many ways throughout my life. Backpacking solo through Europe and the USA in my 20s, buying my first property at 30 and paying it off independently – these were all personal triumphs, especially as a child of conservative migrant parents. As a woman of colour, I also made my mark at the board level in finance, a world where diversity is often lacking. Publicly embracing my spiritual gifts as a medium and spiritual teacher, in a sceptical world, was another triumph; as was transitioning from the security of excel spreadsheets to become a motivational speaker, another bold and scary career move. And in my 40s, I became an author.

There was always one thing missing of course – someone special to accompany me through life's ups and downs. For many years, I doubted whether it would ever actually happen, but I kept my vision.

And finally, at the age of 44, I found my soulmate and embraced marriage. These achievements may not sound as grand as summiting Everest or saving someone's life, but they are my quiet victories, important milestones I *always* envisioned for my life. They didn't align with society's timeline, but I never wavered from the greater vision I had for my life.

The key is to be stubborn with your vision, but flexible with the plan. For this, we need a vision board.

Vision boards

'Thoughts become things. If you see it in your mind, you will hold it in your hand.'

– BOB PROCTOR

Our lives are often so noisy and distracted by the constant buzz of social media. It's like we're drowning in a sea of notifications and endless scrolling, losing touch with our true selves. We are busy with unimportant but urgent tasks. We need help with dreaming big. In fact, dreaming huge and holding that vision despite the noise in our lives. This is where a visual roadmap can guide us through the chaos and keep our eyes on the prize. This tool is a vision board.

As you embark on the journey of creating your own vision board, I want you to get real with yourself. Get self-centred, get honest, and amplify the vision you have for your life. Challenge those sneaky little thoughts that tell you:

'I can't be a mum and run a business.'

'I can't start a new job and explore dating.'

'I can't have a baby past the age of 40.'

Don't let any nasty 'too's' hold you back − you know, the ones that whisper:

'Too old!'

'Too hard!'

'Too poor!'

'Too busy!'

'Too risky!'

Your vision board is your canvas, so paint it with the colours of possibility.

Make sure your vision board covers all the bases. In my experience coaching women, I've noticed certain patterns. Corporate high-flyers often neglect their dating lives (yes − that included me). Working mums put self-care and holidays on the back burner. Older women shy away from online dating, while younger clients worry about time running out to start a family.

My advice? Forget about timelines, financial constraints, or what others might think. Focus on the essentials: family, career, health, spirituality, fitness, mindset and wealth − what they mean for you, in your own time and in your own unique way. And don't forget to include special sections for your birthday, holidays, key relationships, breaking through limiting beliefs and acquiring new skills. Your vision board is your personal roadmap for you to chart in the most authentic way possible.

It is important to review and update your vision board regularly, whether it's on a monthly or fortnightly basis. Make this *Little Brave Act* of creating a vision board a habit. The act of updating your vision board is like checking in with your soul. It's asking yourself, 'Is this still what I want? Have I discovered new desires, new paths I want to explore?' As you continue to evolve and grow through your inner work, your goals and visions may shift accordingly. By keeping your vision board current, you ensure that it reflects your ever-changing aspirations and desires, keeping them at the forefront of your mind. This practice not only reinforces your commitment to your dreams, but also allows you to stay aligned with the path you're forging for yourself.

Before I met and married my husband, my vision board depicted a joyful family with two young children. That didn't change once I married, nor when we agreed to try IVF, given our ages and difficulty in conceiving.

When we first began that journey, I never anticipated it would stretch over nearly three years, but for all that time my vision board had that joyful family with two young children at its heart.

During the first year of IVF, I also adorned it with images of radiant pregnant women, hopeful and expectant. But as we encountered hurdles along the way, I updated the board with pictures of resilient women navigating the IVF injection process, supported by their partners.

It's essential to cling to our ultimate vision while remaining flexible and receptive to the journey's twists and turns. Our vision boards must evolve alongside us, reflecting the changes we're willing to embrace.

Whenever I gaze at my own vision board, I spend a moment with my eyes closed to immerse myself in the scene unfolding before me, turning it into a vivid action-filled movie within my mind. This visualisation exercise is, in my opinion, the most crucial part of the process. As I delve into this mental imagery, I feel a surge of positive emotions – excitement, joy, anticipation – all beginning to stir within me. With each passing moment, the visualisation becomes increasingly vibrant and lifelike, as if I'm watching a movie playing out in my imagination.

Our vision is not what we see with our eyes open.
It is what we see when our eyes are closed.

Through this practice, I'm not merely wishing for my dreams to come true; I'm actively training my body and mind to expect their realisation. It's a shift from mere hope and desire to a sense of certainty – a powerful secret ingredient in the manifestation process.

At the end of this chapter is a simple visualisation script to read and use to support you with bringing your vision to life.

Vision words

'Even miracles take a little time.'

– FAIRY GODMOTHER, *CINDERELLA*

While vision boards are one tool to help you focus on your dreams, focusing on a word-for-the-year is another. Choosing a word-for-the-year isn't just a trendy practice – it's a powerful tool for intentional living. This word becomes our North Star, guiding our decisions, actions, and priorities with clarity and purpose. It's a reminder to stay focused on what truly matters to us, even when life gets chaotic or overwhelming. Whether that word is 'courage', 'gratitude' or 'surrender', our word-of-the-year grounds us in our values and nudges us towards growth and transformation. It's a simple yet profound practice that empowers us to live with intention, authenticity and alignment.

Even the little step of choosing a word-for-the-year is a way of working with the universe to support the changes and growth needed at any particular time.

In the cycle of life, the universe wants us to focus on the big stuff and not cloud our already difficult healing journey, which is where your word-for-the-year can truly find its power. But perhaps you don't want to be limited to one word? If so, I invite you to reflect on past years of your life, and to recognise the primary theme of each year. This will help you to reflect on the years ahead, and what primary theme you want them to have, each in turn.

The year I met my husband, my own word-for-the-year was 'miracles'. I will be honest – I was desperate. Usually, I start contemplating my word-for-the-year in the preceding October. I believe that energetic shifts happen well before 1 January. But that year, there were so many changes I wanted for my life I was at a loss choosing a single word that could hold the transformation I was seeking.

Well into my 40s, I strongly suspected the relationship I was in was not going to last (the one just before my book launch). I also wanted a sea change, to live near a beach and move away from my home in the middle of the city. With my book about to launch, I still felt like an imposter as an author and a speaker, so wanted that to change too. And, of course, I still deeply wished for a soulmate relationship and a child.

I remember speaking out loud one day, 'I need so many miracles to happen next year!'

Just like that, I knew that my word was 'miracle'.

And it worked!

I have chosen a range of words over the years, and it's consistently astounding how they've shaped my experiences. The year I chose 'abundance', my business revenue doubled. When 'forgiveness' was my focus, I witnessed profound shifts in my family relationships. And with 'community' as my word, I found myself surrounded by friends, support and social gatherings.

Of course, when I settled on 'miracle', I didn't fully grasp what I was inviting into my life. Upon reflection, in some ways it was an act of surrender. I was saying to the universe, 'My life is in a bit of a mess, I need some help. Can I outsource this year to you?'

As you now know, I left that unhealthy romantic relationship, paving the way for a fresh chapter. As my book launched, so many other opportunities presented themselves, providing me a platform to address imposter syndrome and amplify my message to the world. I met my husband later that year and we started our IVF journey. Then, in December, the production company of the reality documentary series titled Big Miracles reached out.

The power of one word!

What will be your word-for-the-year?

When I work with clients these are the types of words that have served as a guiding light for their year. Consider words such as courage, healing, joy, resilience, gratitude, growth, balance, love, empower, transform, bold, peace, abundance, clarity, freedom, strength, faith, harmony, adventure, presence, inspire, simplify, thrive, connect and renew. Each word holds the potential to shape your journey, to guide your actions and to inspire you throughout the year.

Whatever visioning tools you use to bravely craft your vision and support you on your path, know that they will be an essential part of the process to ensure you feel empowered, to define and clarify the elements of your vision, and help you move on from your initial path (Plan A) and your compromised path (Plan B) towards the next part of your bigger and better life, the unexpected path: Plan C.

Getting what we ask for

'The universe doesn't distinguish between good and bad.
It only gives you what you focus on.'

– GABRIELLE BERNSTEIN

I once had a boyfriend who was obsessed with his guru, followed his every word like it was gospel. The funny thing? I turned around and made my boyfriend my guru, following him just as blindly. There I was, in a dysfunctional spiritual love triangle trying to figure out why I was suddenly meditating at 5 am and drinking kale smoothies.

Over time, I realised our relationship was built on imbalance, sacrifice and different dreams. I wanted a child; he didn't. And let's be clear, there's absolutely nothing wrong with not wanting children. But staying in a relationship where our visions for the future were completely misaligned? That's a recipe for disaster.

I thought I could change him. I twisted myself into knots, did emotional backflips and contorted myself into someone I wasn't, all in the hope that he would eventually embrace fatherhood and marriage. But here's the truth: you can't bend yourself out of shape to fit someone else's mould and expect it to last.

It was a time in my life where, rather than doing *Little Brave Acts,* I was mired in *Big Acts of Denial*.

One day over lunch, I declared to him and the universe (because you know the universe is always listening), 'I would love to stand on the Love Lock Bridge in Paris on Valentine's Day.' I was nudging him towards a wedding proposal, thinking, wouldn't that just be the perfect place? The Love Lock Bridge, famous for lovers placing padlocks on its fencing, symbolising their unbreakable bond. It seemed like the ultimate gesture of locked-in love. But looking back, I see I was more in love with the idea of love than with the reality of our mismatched dreams. I was completely swept up in the romance of romance.

I chanted Hare Krishna, gave up meat, embraced a vegan lifestyle and went on this wild mission with him seeking enlightenment. The irony is that those days can be pretty dark when you're chasing enlightenment with the wrong person and for all the wrong reasons. I shapeshifted myself into someone I wasn't, hoping to find something real, but all I found was more confusion and disconnection from my true self.

Eighteen months into our relationship, and my birthday was just around the corner. I was about to turn 38, that infamous number everyone loves to remind you about when they talk about fertility falling off a cliff. I decided enough was enough and insisted he commit to having a family. But instead of stepping up, he picked up his feet, turned around and walked away. Just like that. It was a harsh reminder that, sometimes, the act of standing up for what you need means letting go of what you thought you wanted.

My boss could see that I was a mess. I went from being a high-performing employee to a walking zombie, living off coffee and heartbreak. A month after my break-up, she called me into her office. 'Would you like to go to Paris?' It was the end of January, and my work schedule was wide open. My eyes lit up, 'Definitely.'

'It will be quite cold, and you'll be leaving the Sydney summer behind, but there's a finance conference I'd like you to attend.'

Three weeks later, I found myself standing on the Love Lock Bridge on Valentine's Day, tears streaming down my face. I was single, not an engagement ring in sight, and clutching a hot water bottle to stay warm. There I was, in the city of love, facing the raw reality of my heartache. It wasn't the fairytale I once dreamed of, but it was real. And in that moment, I embraced the cold, harsh truth that my vision lacked clarity and honesty.

The universe has a wild sense of humour, and believe me, she listens. I had asked the universe to let me stand on the Love Lock Bridge on Valentine's Day, no mention of a soulmate with a life path that aligned with mine. I manifested exactly what I asked for, but the universe doesn't judge what's good or bad for you. She simply delivers what we think we deserve. What we ask for.

My vision wasn't aligned with the true longings of my soul, and so the universe handed me a lesson wrapped in misery, showing me just how off-track I was. It was like she was saying, 'You wanted this? Here, take it, and let's see how it feels.' I had to face the brutal truth: my dreams were completely out of whack with my real desires. The universe was practically screaming at me to get my act together and figure out what I truly wanted.

It was a wake-up call, a divine intervention demanding that I align my vision with my soul's deepest longings. Because when you're not clear and honest with yourself, the universe has a way of shaking things up until you finally are.

Manifesting a vision

'The flower doesn't dream of the bee.
It blossoms and the bee comes.'

– MARK NEPO

So I started the process of manifesting through taking powerful little steps.

In the years that followed, my *Little Brave Act* was to get crystal clear on what I wanted from a relationship and what my non-negotiables were. I was done settling. I needed a man who would support me wholeheartedly in my purpose-led business, who wanted to have children, and who was a perfect blend of athleticism with a love for the arts. I craved someone with a big, warm, generous heart and the exact quirky sense of humour that could match my own. I pulled together over 10 different manifestation lists I had scribbled down over the years, and you know what? I realised these five things were the essence of what I truly wanted. The rest of my lists? Just noise. Fluff. Distractions. My heart knew what really mattered, and it was about time I listened. This was about aligning with the deepest, truest desires of my soul and refusing to settle for anything less.

Manifesting is about getting clear.

The little step I took was to take a hard look at where I wasn't embodying these qualities in my own life. I got fitter, dedicated myself more fully to my business, and worked on opening my heart to my friends and family. I realised I had become too serious, so I made it a priority to bring fun, play and joy back into my life. Bit by bit, I started to transform. This momentum of change began to build, and I could feel myself aligning more closely with the person I wanted to be and the partner I wanted to attract.

Manifesting is about becoming the things we want to manifest.

I was surrounded by girlfriends who didn't believe in dating apps. They were convinced all the good guys were already married, and the single ones came with complicated ex-wives and no desire for children. The older guys wanted younger women, and the younger guys were only looking for flings. The limitations in our thinking could have gone on forever.

My next little step was to believe. One day, I decided to declare my truth (and you know the universe was listening). 'I just want one guy – my guy. I know he's out there. I'm done with ghosting and lessons. I finally know my worth, and I believe I'm worthy of meeting him. Bring him to me as quickly as possible. I am ready.'

Manifesting requires us to believe in the unbelievable.

It was a simple, powerful declaration, spoken with the fierce certainty that comes from finally understanding my own value. And then, just to make sure the universe got the memo, I added a postscript:

'Give me a clear sign that it's him when I see him.'

It wasn't about desperation; it was about clarity. My final little step in this *Little Brave Act* was to believe that the universe would provide me with a clear sign. It was about standing in my power and demanding what my soul knew I deserved. And in that moment, I felt the shift. The universe, with her quirky sense of humour and impeccable timing, was about to deliver.

When manifesting, the universe likes
simple statements that we declare.

I downloaded the Bumble app on my phone. I created an honest, raw profile, stripped of all pretence, and then I waited. I swiped left and right like a maestro conducting the symphony of my love life, and then I waited some more. Almost instantly, Tyson messaged me back. His profile looked almost too good to be true – no baggage, a big, beautiful warm smile, an actor who loved the arts, and a guy who ran ultramarathons. He was my list in human form.

As I swiped through his photos, one picture stood out. He was standing in front of a big red hut in a stunning and remote part of Australia, well-known for its hiking. My heart skipped a beat. I texted him back immediately, 'I recognise the hut in your photo. Is that Valentine's Hut?'

Ping. His reply was almost instant, 'Yes, that is Valentine's Hut. I was there on New Year's Eve.'

As I read his message, I scratched my head and typed back, 'I was there on New Year's Eve too!'

He replied, 'I was camping above the hut. We must have just missed each other. Wow!!!!'

I inhaled deeply as a smile spread across my face. This was it. This was my sign – a sliding door moment. The universe, with her impeccable timing and sense of humour, had delivered. Here he was – my guy.

> *You will get a sign and often more than one, in the process of manifesting.*

I wanted a special moment on Valentine's Day, a picture-perfect scene that my heart wasn't fully aligned with. Instead, the universe gave me something even more profound – a special moment with a man I almost met eight months earlier near a hut called, fittingly enough, 'Valentine's'.

In the end, I got my Valentine. It took 10 more years, but I held onto my vision and surrendered to the timing. I trusted that when the universe was ready, it would deliver. And it did, in its own perfect, messy, beautiful way. Because sometimes, what we think we want is just a shadow of what we truly need. And when we align our vision with our hearts, the universe has a way of bringing us exactly what we're meant to have.

After our first date, Tyson and I moved faster than a Kardashian marriage. We were living together after just five weeks of dating. Within three months, we were already diving into the world of IVF. It was like we were on a speed date with destiny, but hey, when you know, you know. Plus, who doesn't love a good whirlwind romance with a side of hormone injections?

Simple visualisation script

Close your eyes, take a deep breath, and allow yourself to sink into the comfort of this moment. Let all the worries and distractions of the day melt away as you bring your focus inward. Feel the gentle rise and fall of your breath, the steady rhythm that connects you to the present. Now, imagine standing in front of your large, beautiful vision board. This board is a reflection of your heart's deepest desires, the dreams you hold for your future. See the images, the words and the colours that represent everything you wish to manifest.

With your eyes still closed, let's take a journey into this vision board. Picture yourself stepping into the board, becoming part of the vibrant, living canvas. Feel the energy of your dreams surrounding you, enveloping you in warmth and light.

Look around and see the images coming to life. There's a photo of a joyful family gathering. Picture yourself there, surrounded by your loved ones, feeling the love and connection that fills the space. Hear the laughter, see the smiles, and feel the deep sense of belonging and harmony.

Shift your focus to an image of your dream career. Visualise yourself thriving in this role, using your unique gifts and talents to make a meaningful impact. See the satisfaction and pride in your work, the respect and appreciation from colleagues and clients. Feel the excitement and fulfilment that comes from doing what you love.

Now, move to an image representing your health and wellness. Picture yourself in a state of vibrant health, your body strong and your mind clear. See yourself engaging in activities that bring you joy and vitality, whether it's a morning run, a yoga session or a peaceful walk in nature. Feel the energy and well-being radiating from within.

There's an image of a beautiful, serene place that represents your spiritual connection. Visualise yourself in this sacred space, feeling deeply connected to the divine, to your inner wisdom and to the universe. Feel the peace, the clarity and the sense of purpose that comes from this connection.

Now, focus on an image of abundance and wealth. Picture yourself living a life of financial freedom and security. See the ways in which abundance flows to you effortlessly, supporting all your dreams and endeavours. Feel the gratitude and confidence that comes from knowing you are provided for, that you have all you need and more.

Take a moment to let all these images blend together, creating a powerful tapestry of your future. Feel the emotions associated with each vision – joy, love, fulfilment, peace, abundance. Know that these feelings are a sign that you are in alignment with your highest good.

As you slowly start to bring your awareness back to the present moment, know that you carry the energy of these visions within you. Open your eyes, take another deep breath, and let the light of your dreams guide you forward, knowing that you are on the path to manifesting a life that reflects the true desires of your heart.

You are the creator of your reality. Trust in your vision, believe in your dreams and watch as the universe conspires to bring them into your experience.

Brave truths

- When we let go of fixed plans, it's crucial to dream big and boldly, creating a clear, purposeful vision for our lives.

- When we have our own vision, we are more likely to experience positive, goal-oriented stress (eustress) rather than negative, overwhelming stress (distress).

- Creating and regularly updating a vision board helps us dream big and stay focused on our true aspirations, breaking through limiting beliefs and aligning our goals with our evolving desires.

- Choosing a word-for-the-year provides a powerful tool for intentional living, guiding decisions and encouraging *Little Brave Acts* with clarity and purpose.

- Manifesting a vision involves getting clear on our true desires, embodying those qualities in ourselves, believing in the unbelievable, and making powerful and simple declarations to the universe.

Brave questions

- What single word encapsulates your intentions and aspirations for the year ahead? Why does this word resonate with you?

- What do you truly want to manifest in your life this year? Where is your vision lacking? Where are you not dreaming big enough for yourself?

- What limiting beliefs or fears do you need to release to fully embrace your vision for the year?

- How do you want to feel throughout this year? What emotions and states of being do you want to cultivate?

- What *Little Brave Acts* can you take daily or weekly to move closer to your vision and make it a reality?

Brave mantra

I see my vision clearly and trust in the journey.

CHAPTER 7

The powerful little step of self-love

'To love oneself is the beginning of a lifelong romance.'

– OSCAR WILDE

To embrace our vision, let go of plans that don't serve us – to create a life filled with big miracles – we must embrace the profound need for self-love. Self-love is about freeing ourselves from the relentless pursuit of validation and acceptance from others. It involves recognising that our worth isn't up for debate – it's inherent, undeniable and doesn't require anyone else's stamp of approval.

It's in loving ourselves fiercely and unapologetically that we find the courage to break free from societal expectations and trust our inner compass. Embracing self-love means honouring both our external and internal bodies, recognising that our physical appearance and our internal health are worthy of love, respect and care. But let's be honest – self-love is elusive and unknown for many of us, and it will take a *Little Brave Act* to start loving ourselves. Before we talk about how we start, let's address the common experience of many women. Let's start with hating ourselves a little less.

The challenge of self-love

'How you love yourself is how you teach others to love you.'

– RUPI KAUR

I used to hate myself. Every day, I would wage a war against my own spirit, putting myself down with negative self-talk. Unhealthy comparisons became my constant companions. When I'd walk into a room, I would find a reason why my peers were better than me, which turned out to be quite easy. I would then proceed to justify why they would not like me and ultimately not be my friend. Sounds like a fun way to exist, right?

Interestingly, I looked like a picture of success on the outside and no one knew my dirty little secret: that I loathed myself. No one had a clue about the battles raging within me. Any one of us can put on a protective armour of bold sassy clothes, or style our hair to be big and voluminous, and we can pretend we're convincing ourselves that we do love ourselves. But it means nothing if deep down we're just trying to hide our perceived flaws.

When friends would tell me I needed to love myself, my initial reaction was always, 'What on earth are you talking about?' It only triggered more self-directed anger and self-loathing, and I added self-love to the long list of things I was not good at that justified my negative sense of self.

Even when I found myself face to face with psychologists, and they would offer me well-meaning platitudes about self-love or ask why I didn't love myself, I would reply, 'I just don't. I don't see what there is to love.'

Rarely did they offer me a diagnosis, a long-term solution, or a circuit breaker that worked, leaving me feeling even more adrift in my struggle. So, for many years, I found myself grappling with this enigmatic concept called 'self-love'.

Finally, after decades of pursuing my own healing journey, I have learned about self-love, and what I have learned has enabled me to guide and support other women. Initially, self-love *is* a mystery. The journey of mastering self-love is like trying to hold water in your hands. I am even reticent to use the word mastery and self-love in the same sentence, as there is no destination or degree that can signal accomplishment. It is a delicate balance between acceptance and transformation.

Self-love beckons us into the depths of our own souls, daring us to confront the stories we've been told about our worthiness, or the ones we have made up about ourselves, and rewrite them with courage and compassion. It's a journey of constant unravelling, an ongoing process of shedding the layers of shame and self-doubt that have held us back for far too long. Self-love challenges us to embrace the fullness of our humanity – the messy, imperfect, gloriously human parts of ourselves – and to love fiercely, despite it all.

Initially, loving yourself will feel like an act of revolution.

Self-love is a radical act of rebellion against the norms and expectations that society tries to impose upon us. It might not always be immediately obvious, but the truth is we often find ourselves hating who we are because of the relentless pressure from our environment, our culture, our families and yes, even our Instagram feeds. We're bombarded with images and messages telling us what 'perfect', 'aspirational' and 'successful' look like, and we internalise these standards, projecting them onto our chaotic, beautifully imperfect lives.

But loving ourselves unapologetically? That's like waving a flag of defiance in the face of societal expectations. When we buy into these expectations and inevitably fall short, it's a slippery slope into self-hatred.

So what if you still have cellulite after trying every diet in the book? So what if you went back to work 'too soon' after having children? So what if you're dating casually after a divorce? So what if you turn down that job offer everyone else thinks is perfect? Don't let it get to you!

Each day, strive to hate yourself a little less and love yourself a little more.

When we don't fit into the mould society has carved out for us, yet we desperately want to, we betray ourselves with self-hate, and it limits our vision of the future.

How to silence self-hate

'Navigating self-hate is about recognizing that the cruel voices in your head are not telling the truth about who you are.'

– LOUISE HAY

I have found that the journey to loving ourselves is not passive and gentle – it's a revolutionary act that requires a defiant mindset. We need to summon up a *Little Brave Act*, harnessing an oppositional force within us to break free from the confines of conformity. It's about reclaiming our power, our autonomy and our right to exist exactly as we are.

The journey starts with the little step of seeking out new role models – individuals who embody authenticity, resilience *and* self-love. We need to become discerning with our social media consumption, curating our feeds to include content that uplifts and inspires, rather than content that instigates comparison and self-doubt. It's also about choosing wisely who we engage in soul-baring conversations with, surrounding ourselves with those who support and encourage our growth.

And let's not forget the importance of shutting out the noise of life that doesn't serve us – whether it's negative self-talk, toxic relationships or societal expectations that weigh us down.

This is how we begin to create a new frame of reference, shifting our mindset and rewriting the narrative about who we are and what we're capable of achieving.

Society often dictates that success is measured by status, wealth and power. But self-love whispers a different truth.

Shannon Kaiser, in *The Self-Love Experiment*, reminds us that self-love is an ongoing journey, not a destination. She writes, 'Self-love is showing up for yourself even when you feel unworthy, especially when you feel unworthy.' This means taking small brave, consistent actions to honour your needs and desires, even when it feels difficult. It's about embracing your imperfections and understanding that you are enough, just as you are.

When I run my online spiritual courses, I find myself staring into the eyes of many corporate women, their faces alight with curiosity and longing as they sip from the cup of my own empowered truths. They sit at their desks on lunchbreaks, yearning for something more, for something deeper than the confines of their corporate roles. Many of them arrive carrying the heavy burdens of self-hate and its cousin, self-guilt, for even daring to consider a life beyond the corporate grind. They've invested countless hours, energy and money into their careers, but deep down, they know there's something missing.

As the weeks progress, and I share my own radical journey of leaving behind my corporate executive job as a finance director to pursue my calling as a psychic medium and spiritual teacher, something shifts within them. They begin to see the potential for their own transformation, their own journey towards alignment with their passion and purpose. I show them that there's another way – a path less travelled, perhaps, but one that leads to fulfilment and authenticity.

It's about veering off the beaten path, choosing a less conventional route, and daring to pursue work that aligns with your deepest passions and values. And in doing so, you discover that true success isn't measured by external markers, but by the depth of fulfilment and joy you find in following your heart.

Self-love is about recognising that our worthiness doesn't hinge on anyone else's approval or validation. In relationships, self-love is also a game-changer. Society loves to tell us that our worth is tied to our ability to attract and keep a partner, even if it comes at the cost of our own well-being. But self-love? It flips the script entirely. When we prioritise our own happiness, we walk away from relationships that no longer serve or uplift us, and we make ourselves open to new beginnings.

> *There will always be someone who does not see your worth. Don't let it be you!*

As the years passed, I took my own powerful little step of hating myself just a little less. When we do that, we nudge ourselves in the direction of self-love. The next step is to predict the hurdles that get in the way of feeling self-love, so we can overcome them.

Navigating hurdles

'Loving yourself isn't vanity; it's sanity.'

– KATRINA MAYER

Every time I found myself ending a relationship, it wasn't the conversation with the partner at the time that would overwhelm me with feelings of self-hate or despair. No, it was the conversation I anticipated having with my parents that I dreaded.

You see, I come from a conservative Sri Lankan culture where the path to love is prescriptive and well defined. You meet someone, you date for a respectable period of time, swiftly get engaged, before you find out too much about each other's flaws, and throw a grand wedding. Then live happily (or not) ever after.

But since I found myself navigating a conga line of suitors, I couldn't help but feel like a disappointment to my parents. I feared they would think I was 'too easy' and 'not discerning enough'. My lack of self-love stemmed from my fear of their judgment, their disapproval and their disappointment, all wrapped up in the expectations of a culture, which I had inherited like a precious heirloom. It felt both familiar and stifling.

Even if you are not from a conservative culture, the aftermath of a break-up can still trigger feelings of self-doubt and inadequacy. You find yourself uttering phrases like, 'I'm back to being single again,' as if being single is somehow wrong, as if you're a societal outcast. Society places such high value on the destination of marriage that the process of navigating in and out of singledom becomes scrutinised and judged.

How do we overcome the hurdles that stand in the way of self-love, those niggles of self-hate that trip us up?

For me, this involved distancing myself from the weight of my parents' expectations, investing less in the tone of their voices and reading less between the lines. Instead, I turned inward, asking myself the important questions:

How can I make different choices next time?

How can I truly listen to and act on the red flags?

This is what self-love looked like for me – a journey of introspection, growth and learning to trust myself above all else. And, once I learned to predict when I might become vulnerable to self-hate, I was able to increase my self-talk to overcome it.

In a world that often demands conformity to expectations, it's a *Little Brave Act* to embrace one's true self.

Emma's powerful little step: confronting inner demons

'I'm really happy to be me, and I'd like to think people like me more because I'm happy with myself and not because I refuse to conform to anything.'

– ADELE

When we anchor our sense of value to the opinions and judgments of others, we become trapped in a cycle of seeking external validation, forever at the mercy of others' perceptions.

'Are you looking forward to our high school reunion?' I gently asked Emma, knowing full well the weight behind my question. Emma was both an ex-schoolmate and a recent client.

She sighed. As we sat shoulder-to-shoulder, devoid of the pressure of eye contact, a safe space for vulnerability and honesty unfolded between us. 'I felt so inadequate in high school,' she confessed. 'I constantly compared myself to other girls. I was probably the largest girl in the year. Most days, I just looked at everyone else and wished I could be them. I didn't even go to our Year 12 formal because I couldn't bear the thought of facing rejection, of asking someone to come with me and hearing them say no.'

Listening to Emma's words, I couldn't help but feel a pang of recognition. We had both battled crippling low self-esteem during our high school years, albeit for different reasons. And yet, in the midst of our struggles, neither of us had been aware of the inner demons the other was facing.

It was a poignant reminder of the silent battles so many of us fight, unseen and unheard, as we navigate the tumultuous waters of adolescence.

'I felt like I had to be the funny one,' Emma continued, her words heavy with the weight of past insecurities. 'The loud one, the outrageous one. It was my way of masking how inadequate I felt. I'd poke fun at my weight before anyone else had the chance to, thinking if I got in first, they wouldn't need to.'

I nodded, because I too had resorted to self-deprecating humour as a shield against my own insecurities, making jokes about my buck teeth, my unfeminine facial hair, my too-brown skin. We had both honed our senses of humour and quick wit into solid armour to survive the trials of high school. Yet, unfortunately, these coping mechanisms persisted long beyond those formative years.

'When did your weight loss journey begin?' I enquired, my curiosity piqued as I searched for Emma's pivotal moment of self-love. I had assumed, perhaps too hastily, that losing the weight would mean she now loved herself.

'So many years later,' she reflected, 'I saw my endocrinologist and she looked me straight in the eye and said, "You're not going to see your son turn eighteen." He was two years old at the time; my daughter was six.'

It was the reality of facing an early death that changed things for Emma.

'One day, randomly, a friend reached out, an acquaintance really, and said, "I am running this thing, this program with Isagenix, and I think it would be great for you." I was like, go away, I don't want to deal with this. I actively tried to avoid her, which was hard, as our daughters were in the same class. She was relentless. I finally caved and said "yes" just to get her off my back.

'Reluctantly, I started the program,' Emma admitted. 'When she asked me how much weight I wanted to lose in thirty days, I threw out a random number: five kilos. It was a goal I didn't truly believe I could reach. But as I started the program and began drinking the shakes, something strange happened. I could feel my blood coursing through my veins, an energy pulsing through me like never before. So, I stuck with it, because I was intrigued by this newfound sensation.

'When I saw my sisters, a few weeks later,' Emma continued, 'I was down eight kilos, and they were incredibly complimentary. Within thirty days, I had lost ten kilos – double my initial goal. It was like a ripple effect, a momentum had started. Suddenly, so many people started reaching out with positive comments.'

'Did you start to love yourself then?' I asked her pointedly.

'Not quite,' Emma replied with a hint of hesitation. 'I think all of the compliments provided a catalyst to keep going and not quit. I still felt the need to hide. I didn't do any exercise, as I didn't want anyone to see me walking or doing exercise. It wasn't until six weeks in that I realised I needed to move my body. I started going for walks at nine o'clock at night, wearing all black, so no one could see me.'

This was an important *Little Brave Act* that Emma embraced in the darkness of her evenings. Her commitment to exercising and persevering with the program was an act of defiance and discipline. Another little step – not quitting. She was hating herself less, the sands were slowly shifting for her, but as I listened to Emma's words, I could sense that at that time she was still grappling with self-love.

'I had a follow-up appointment with my endocrinologist,' Emma recounted. 'During the appointment I was still wearing my Covid mask, so she could not see the transformation right away. But when I removed it, her reaction was priceless. "Holy shit, what's happened to you?" she exclaimed, stunned by the change. She collected her thoughts, then said, "You don't realise what you have done in terms of adding years back to your life." Her acknowledgment was a powerful realisation of the progress I had made.'

After four months Emma decided to post a before and after photo on her social media. 'The response was overwhelming – over 300 positive comments flooded in. I was blown away. Even strangers in my local shopping centre began approaching me. They would say, 'I don't know you, but I've seen you around, and what you have done is incredible!'

You might think that, at this point, Emma had reached the pinnacle of self-love and this is where the story ends. But the truth is that the economy of thinness starts very early in life. Emma was still in the process of confronting her inner demons and learning to accept and cherish herself unconditionally. She was beginning to emerge from the shadows, finding her voice and becoming visible in the world after so many years of playing small and remaining invisible. Her journey of self-love was far from over – it was just unfolding in new and unexpected ways.

Roxane Gay, the author of *Hunger*, poignantly captures the complex struggle faced by women, particularly those who don't fit society's narrow beauty standards. 'As a woman, as a fat woman, I am not supposed to take up space,' she writes. 'And yet, as a feminist, I am encouraged to believe I can take up space. I live in a contradictory space where I should try to take up space but not too much of it, and not in the wrong way, where the wrong way is any way where my body is concerned.'

Emma, like so many others, found herself navigating this same contradiction. She was learning to take up space in a world that had never allowed her to.

Emma's next revelation caught me off guard. 'The old Emma had to die,' she declared dramatically. 'Eighteen months after losing the weight, I experienced a mental health breakdown. I realised it wasn't just about shedding pounds. What I needed was a holistic transformation, one that encompassed not just the physical, but the spiritual and emotional aspects of my being.'

It was this desire for holistic growth that led Emma to reconnect with me, decades after leaving high school, to explore ways to activate her intuition, connect with her higher self, and change her mindset – all in an effort to build up her spiritual self-esteem.

Self-love is radical in a world that profits from your self-doubt.

Her journey to radical self-love went far beyond just losing weight. It was a journey of profound transformation, one that touched every aspect of her being, a journey of growth and acceptance. One that required many little steps.

'Are you looking forward to our high school reunion?' I asked again.

'I can't wait. I'm super excited,' Emma paused, her expression thoughtful. 'There were a few people at high school I didn't treat as well as I should have because I didn't feel worthy. There's one person in particular, she was in our immediate social group; but then, you know, she had a falling out with one of the other girls, and I kind of went against her as well because I wanted to stay in with the cooler people. That's where my mindset was. I treated her really badly.'

Emma's voice softened as she continued, her sincerity evident. 'I'm wanting to put that right. I'm wanting to acknowledge that and say it was because I was hurting and felt that I needed to stick with these other people to make myself feel better.' She paused, her eyes reflecting a sense of introspection.

'Self-love is forgiving yourself,' she asserted. 'A hallmark of self-love is cultivating a deep sense of compassion, forgiveness and empathy towards oneself. From this point, it's easy to love others.'

Author Roxane Gay's words resonated deeply for me at this point: 'It is a powerful lie to equate thinness with self-worth.'

We also attach our self-worth to the illusions of material possessions, societal status and external validation; but true self-love is about recognising and honouring the inherent worth and dignity within ourselves.

Emma had cultivated a deep sense of compassion, forgiveness and empathy towards herself, and was now able to extend that same love, compassion and empathy to those around her.

Maitri: loving kindness

'The most terrifying thing is to accept oneself completely.'

– CARL JUNG

In Buddhism, there's a beautiful practice called *maitri*, which is all about deep, unconditional self-love and self-acceptance. It's about embracing every part of ourselves – loving who we were before, who we are now, and who we will be in the future. Maitri teaches us to befriend even the parts of ourselves we don't like, the ones we usually criticise or hide away. It's not about striving to become a 'better' version of ourselves; it's about recognising that the fundamentally good version of ourselves is already here, right now. Maitri is about befriending our entire selves, not just the parts we like to show off.

THE POWER OF LITTLE STEPS

Renowned Buddhist teacher Pema Chödrön often talks about maitri in terms of compassion and self-compassion. She emphasises the importance of cultivating maitri as a way to navigate life's challenges with kindness and gentleness towards oneself, and that maitri begins with developing loving-kindness towards ourselves – acknowledging our own suffering and imperfections without judgment. She encourages us to extend this compassion outward, towards others, fostering a deeper connection and understanding of our shared humanity. For Chödrön, maitri isn't just a practice, it's a way of being – a transformative journey towards greater self-awareness, acceptance, and love for ourselves and others.

Emma's story beautifully illustrates the essence of maitri. It's not so much about Emma loving herself after losing weight; it's about how she learned to love herself unconditionally, beyond any external changes. Emma confronted her past self-doubt and unworthiness with courage and grace, embracing her humanity and honouring her journey of growth and self-discovery. Through a few *Little Brave Acts*, Emma embraced the transformative power of maitri, cultivating deep acceptance and love for herself and compassion for others. Her story reminds us that maitri isn't just a destination; it's a journey – a journey of radical self-compassion and unwavering self-love.

Changing perceptions of self

'The most powerful relationship you will ever have is the relationship with yourself.'

– STEVE MARABOLI

I had to undertake a similar journey to move on from my chronic self-loathing, and to find acceptance after my Plan B had so publicly failed in season one of the television show *Big Miracles*.

Oh, how I hated my body for failing me! I hated how confident I had felt taking that pregnancy test, believing myself pregnant, only to be drastically wrong. I even hated how confident I had been freezing my eggs at 38, believing it would act as a reliable backup plan. Yep, that familiar self-hate was back.

This time, though, all the little steps I had taken towards self-love before had left a trace of a muscle memory. I knew I just needed to again take that first little step towards self-love. Then I needed to identify the hurdles that would trip me up. I started by changing my social media feed, curating content I would find helpful and positive. I sought out new role models – women who had successfully fallen pregnant later in life. I was selective about my conversations, and closely monitored my self-talk. After that the *Little Brave Acts* came more easily. I revisited my vision board and I added images that represented not just motherhood, but a life filled with love, purpose and joy

I couldn't change the fact that society expected every woman to be able to conceive their own child; but I could change my perception of who I wanted to be in the future. While the core of my self-hate at the time was infertility, my self-love was bigger than any one thing. I knew that in the future, I wanted to be able to inspire others with my story.

Once you have freed yourself from the limitations inflicted through self-hate, you can start to imagine new possibilities for your life – possibilities that truly align with your authentic self.

Loving our wombs

'To heal the womb is to heal the woman.
To heal the woman is to heal the world.'

– QUEEN AFUA

Let's talk about the profound impact of self-love on our bodies, especially our wombs. When we don't love ourselves, when we carry shame and self-loathing, it's not just our hearts that hurt – our wombs feel it too. Conditions like endometriosis, cysts, polyps, fibroids, infertility and even uterine cancers are more than physical ailments; they are manifestations of deeper wounds, often rooted in the mother wound.

Self-love is crucial during every phase of our reproductive lives – whether we're dealing with our periods or navigating menopause. How often do we treat our periods as inconveniences or speak about menopause with shame and resentment? It's time to shift that narrative. By embracing self-love, we can start to heal these deep-seated wounds and honour the incredible power and wisdom of our bodies.

Bravery in women often starts with acknowledging and nurturing their wombs.

My client Morgan was seeking spiritual, mindset and emotional tools when she started working with me. Sensitive and highly intuitive, I instinctively knew her journey would involve healing her body – especially her womb.

One day, she shared, 'My endo journey was my dark night of the soul. I kept putting on weight, had terrible period pains and knew something had to change. For years, I had undiagnosed endometriosis. I was told it was normal, but what I was experiencing felt so abnormal. I felt unable to speak up.'

We are so conditioned to hate our bodies and dismiss our pain. Yet, endometriosis is our body's way of screaming for attention, begging us to listen, nurture and heal. It's our body saying, 'I need you to love me.' Ignoring this plea perpetuates the cycle of pain, keeping our wombs trapped in dis-ease, echoing the emotional turmoil we've carried for generations.

Morgan's body was screaming, crying and revolting. Her plan to have a family was being disrupted, and it was time to slow down and do the inner work to heal.

Morgan persisted until a doctor finally listened. 'I discovered that I had stage four endometriosis, which had spread to my other organs. It was now on my bladder and diaphragm. During exploratory surgery, they found five large cysts and a mysterious mass. I had to be prepared for cancer.'

Now in her early 30s, Morgan watched her carefully laid plans for her health and family planning unravel. In a session, I shared with Morgan the impacts of the mother wound on our lives and, in her case, on her womb. The *mother wound* is the generational pain passed down from mothers to daughters, teaching us that our worth is tied to how perfectly we can fit into society's expectations. We internalise the belief that we must be smaller, quieter and less needy. This pain settles in our wombs, creating fertile ground for conditions such as endometriosis.

During her healing, Morgan shared, 'A woman came into my dreams and said, "What if you do have cancer, Morgan? Journal about it."' Having resisted her spiritual tools, Morgan realised dream journalling was crucial to her healing journey.

Dream journalling is a powerful way to speak to our unconscious mind. Every night, your subconscious speaks to you in the language of dreams, revealing truths you might not be ready to face in your waking life. It's an act of self-discovery and self-compassion, allowing you to connect with your inner wisdom and understand yourself on a profound level.

As Morgan began dream journalling, she asked herself:

What fears do I have of being a mother?

What was my relationship with my mother like as a child?

What is my womb trying to tell me?

Where am I blocking my feminine side expressing itself?

During her self-inquiry, Morgan remembered her hyper-vigilance as a child growing up in a household where there was a lot of anger and rage between her parents and her mother battled with addiction.

Morgan shared, 'I had to take care of my mother a lot of the time. I recall many times needing to put her to bed because she was so drunk.'

In one session, I asked, 'Are you familiar with the term parentification?' She shook her head.

Parentification is when a child is forced to grow up too fast, taking on the roles and responsibilities of an adult because the adults in their life are not stepping up. It's when a child becomes the caregiver, the emotional support, the problem-solver – essentially, the parent to their own parents or siblings.

Morgan remembers taking care of her siblings and growing up in a fog of instability. She became hyper-vigilant about her mother's feelings, trying to absorb and alleviate her pain. This experience is like being handed a heavy backpack filled with rocks when you're just a kid and being told, 'Carry this, too.' It's an overwhelming burden that strips away the innocence and freedom of childhood. You learn to navigate adult problems with a child's heart. While it can make you resilient and strong, it can also leave scars that take years to understand and heal.

Morgan was taught to be self-reliant and responsible far too early, at the cost of her own needs and dreams. This role reversal disrupts the natural order of things, leaving her to juggle adult duties while still trying to figure out who she is.

As an adult, Morgan became hyper-independent, determined not to let anyone take away her independence or to feel responsible for another person. This is the problematic mindset we adopt when we experience parentification.

When working with Morgan, I felt like I was seeing a mirror of myself. Hyper-independence can produce great success in our careers, yet over time the tall walls Morgan and I had built to protect ourselves had to come crumbling down.

How would romantic love find its way into our closed hearts? Or the tenderness of a child that needed a nurturing mother? At this point in time, I too was searching for love and a child.

Healing from parentification involves acknowledging the weight you've been carrying, understanding that it wasn't yours to bear, and giving yourself permission to reclaim your childhood and your right to be cared for. It's about breaking the cycle and allowing yourself the grace to be imperfect, to need and to receive.

To heal our wombs, we must also heal our hearts. We need to confront the mother wound, acknowledge the pain, and choose a different path. We need to break the cycle, to teach ourselves and our daughters that our bodies are sacred, deserving of love and respect.

How did Morgan do this? She had to reclaim and step into her feminine power. This wasn't about taking the big, bold, masculine steps she was used to — it was about embracing the power of little steps. Morgan began with simple healing tools: she watched funny movies to bring laughter back into her days, took walks in nature, started with short meditations, journalled daily, danced alone in her apartment surrounded by candlelight and practised morning affirmations. She slowed down and tapped into her intuition, allowing herself to heal and grow with each gentle, intentional step.

Morgan began to realise she needed to love all of herself, embracing the Buddhist philosophy of maitri. She listed everything she was grateful for about herself, standing naked in front of a mirror and saying aloud what she loved. She started with the obvious: her beautiful blonde curly hair, her sparkling blue eyes. Then she glanced down at her rounded stomach, which had challenged her for years, and said, 'I love my belly.' She turned her gaze to her womb and finally declared, 'I am grateful for my womb. I am grateful for my endo. I love my endo.' This is what self-love looks like: gratitude for our dis-ease that is helping us heal our minds and emotions.

Self-love must extend to our wombs, including the dis-eases that are speaking to us.

Our bodies are wise. They carry the stories of our ancestors and the power to transform pain into strength. Today, women have the tools and knowledge to heal ourselves. When a woman heals herself, she heals her daughter, her mother and the community around her. Women intuitively understand the importance of healing our wombs, not just for ourselves, but for the collective.

Morgan shared, 'Women can have up to 10 surgeries for endo. I've only needed one, and I plan to not have any more. I also don't have cancer.' As a teacher, watching my students bloom is my greatest joy. The more Morgan listened to her body, the more she realised it was giving her answers not just for healing, but for her purpose and the next steps in her life.

A brave woman listens to the whisper of her womb and honours its wisdom.

As Morgan embraced self-love, she was drawn to advanced healing tools like kinesiology, sound healing and bioresonance. She constantly listened to the creative wisdom of her womb and followed its guidance. She transformed her wounded womb into a source of wisdom and now specialises in helping women heal their womb and their mother wound.

Morgan's journey is a testament to the power of self-love and the magic that happens when we tune into our bodies. Her original plans may have failed, but this unexpected path led her to a deeper purpose. She teaches us that our pain can be our greatest teacher, guiding us to our true calling and helping us heal generations of women by addressing the wounds within ourselves.

When life doesn't go according to plan, it's often because something greater is waiting for us. Our bodies are trying to tell us something, pushing us towards a path we might not have chosen but desperately need. By embracing the unexpected and trusting our inner wisdom, we can start healing our wombs and our deep-seated mother wounds, finding our way to a more meaningful and purpose filled life.

Brave truths

- Self-love is a radical act of reclaiming our inherent worth, independent of anyone else's approval.

- Our worth isn't negotiable; self-love is about accepting that truth and bravely living it every day.

- To practise self-love is to silence the inner critic and amplify the voice of compassion within us. There will always be someone who does not see your worth! Don't let it be you.

- In Buddhism, the practice of maitri emphasises deep, unconditional self-love and acceptance by embracing every part of ourselves, recognising that our fundamentally good self is already present, and extending compassion inward and outward.

- A woman's journey to self-love means embracing her womb, her body, her periods, and the transitions when her periods stop. It's about loving every part of herself, through every season and every change.

Brave questions

- What does loving yourself look like today? How can you show yourself kindness and compassion right now, in this moment?

- When was the last time you spoke kindly to yourself? Or kindly to your womb? Reflect on your inner dialogue. Are you your own best friend or your harshest critic?

- What are the small things you appreciate about yourself? List five qualities or actions that you love about who you are.

- Think about someone who embodies self-love. What can you learn from their approach to themselves?

- What negative beliefs about yourself are you ready to let go of? Identify one or two limiting beliefs that no longer serve you. How can you begin to release them?

Brave mantra

I am enough, just as I am. I choose to love myself
bravely and unapologetically.

CHAPTER 8

The powerful little step of setting boundaries

'Every woman that finally figured out her worth, has picked up her suitcases of pride and boarded a flight to freedom, which landed in the valley of change.'

SHANNON L. ALDER

We now have a vision in place and the self-love to bravely step into that vision. Yet, as we open ourselves to the possibility of new ways to live a fulfilling life, we often find a heavy, familiar feeling creeping in: the fear of being selfish. It's like an unwelcome guest that shows up just when we're about to do something courageous and true to ourselves.

To continue onwards, we have to take the *Litte Brave Act* of setting boundaries. Boundaries that will support our forward momentum and protect our path. Boundaries are the guardians of our dreams. Yet, setting boundaries often feels like an act of defiance. Yes, we're making new decisions for ourselves, and that's exactly why it feels so daunting. This uncomfortable feeling can easily lure us away from prioritising moving forward, tempting us to revert to our old patterns, putting others first instead. But let's be clear: this only delays what's meant for us.

Setting boundaries has always been a struggle for me. And guess what? I don't know many who've got boundary-setting all figured out. It's like women were given a manual for everything except 'How to Say No Without Feeling Guilty'. From the time we're young girls, we're bombarded with messages about putting others' needs before our own, about being the perfect nurturers, the perfect pleasers. We're conditioned to believe that our worth hinges on how much we can sacrifice for others.

Somewhere along the way, we lose sight of our own needs, our own desires. We forget that it's not just okay, but absolutely necessary, to honour ourselves first. And so we find ourselves saying 'yes' when we mean 'no', then wonder why we're left feeling drained and depleted, or with a vague sense of feeling lost in our life. It's not that we don't want to set boundaries; it's just that nobody ever showed us how.

We need to be able to set boundaries in order to reclaim our power and purpose. The journey of mastering this art of boundaries begins with one small, courageous step – the powerful little step of self-respect.

Now, let me be honest: this is no walk in the park. Well, it hasn't been for me. But it's absolutely essential on our journey towards healing and authenticity. At some point in our adult lives, every single one of us needs to learn how to set boundaries.

Types of boundaries

These are the different types of boundaries. Some need to be a high brick wall topped with barbed wire, while others are more like a line in the sand.

The boundaries that usually first spring to mind are what I like to call the boundaries of the 'hard no'. These arise in sticky situations like toxic romantic relationships, being bullied by friends, or being taken advantage of financially. These are the big teaching moments that smack us in the face when we've ignored the universe's gentle nudges to set boundaries for too long. The 'hard no' boundary tends to be born out of crisis. We struggle here if our primary caretakers didn't show us the ropes when it came to healthy boundaries. In fact, we may have been shown the opposite: sacrifice, subjugation, smallness. Without a good role model, we have no idea how to set boundaries for ourselves. Until we learn to set 'hard no' boundaries, their absence will serve as roadblocks getting in the way of us fulfilling our vision.

Then there are the boundaries that pit us against authority figures. These often stem from entrenched relationships – such as family, bosses, colleagues – where the power dynamic is set-up from the outset. Asserting our needs becomes a crucial part of adulting and boundaries will need to be addressed at some point, even though it might be uncomfortable. We struggle here with boundaries because, let's be honest, relating to authority – a parent, a boss – in a healthy way isn't exactly second nature to most of us.

Everyone's needs may be different, so the only way to co-exist and thrive within these relationships is by speaking up. It's about knowing when to draw the line and stand firm in our convictions, even if it feels uncomfortable. Until we learn to set authority boundaries, their absence will hold us back.

Then there are the boundaries that arise within the dance of friendship, the 'evolving boundaries', where we're navigating the ever-changing tides of growth and authenticity. We stumble here because we prefer to endure discomfort rather than risk hurting a beloved friend. It's about honouring both our own evolution and that of our dear loving friends, and finding harmony as we each strive towards becoming more fully ourselves within the relationship. Thus, we learn to honour and value another person's needs and ours at the same time, while maintaining the joy and fulfilment that the relationship provides. Until we learn to set friendship boundaries, their absence will make our journeys harder.

Let's not forget the inner boundaries – the ones that require discipline, energy management and self-care. These are the non-negotiables that keep us grounded, ensuring our lives are filled with purpose and fulfilment. These types of boundaries are about committing to the gym instead of hitting the snooze button at 6 am or resisting the temptation of online shopping so we can meet our monthly savings goal, or prioritising sleep over mindless scrolling on social media. We falter here because delayed gratification isn't exactly our forte, and we're still in the process of forming habits and reaping the rewards of having them in place.

These inner boundaries are also about what we will and won't accept in order to honour what is right for us, especially in the face of seismic changes like divorce and separation. They come into play when dealing with career changes such as deciding to leave a toxic job that's draining your spirit. They're crucial when navigating health challenges and choosing to put your well-being first even when it's inconvenient or unpopular. They guide us in managing family dynamics, helping us set limits with loved ones to protect our peace and sanity. Inner boundaries are about saying 'no' to what drains us and 'yes' to what nourishes us. It's about standing firm in our values and knowing that protecting our inner peace is just as important as setting external limits.

Lastly, there's the art of being okay when others set boundaries with us. Here it's about embracing the fact that everyone has their own needs and limits, and that respecting those boundaries is an act of love and understanding. We stumble here when we haven't quite mastered setting our own boundaries. It's easy to feel resentful and bitter when others have learned this skill and we're still playing catch-up. Adopting the mindset that learning about boundaries is both messy and beautiful and we're all in it together will allow us to learn from others and not be victims in this process.

When I first became aware that I needed to put more boundaries in place, like many women, I thought boundaries were solely about the 'hard no' boundary, leaving no room for anything else. This myth about boundary-setting held me back from more thoroughly understanding this important topic. I thought I had to be aggressive and selfish to set boundaries, using them as walls to keep people at arm's length. I lived under the illusion that everyone in the world was out to take advantage of me, so my default mode became putting up boundaries with anyone who crossed my path.

I even bought into the idea that friendships had to end and estrangement from family was the only solution when a boundary was breached. Can you imagine? I went from feeling disrespected, ignored and fearful due to a lack of boundaries, to feeling angry, bitter, resentful and utterly alone with them in place. People stopped trying to connect with me, no one knew the real me, and I alienated loved ones.

Over time, I came to realise there had to be a healthy middle ground, a way to set boundaries without being so polarising, and I set out to find what that might be.

Establishing the limit

'Those who get angry when you set a boundary
are the ones you need to set boundaries for.'

– J.S. WOLFE, *THE PATHOLOGY OF INNOCENCE*

When we are slow in learning our lessons, the universe will deliver us with the mother of all teachings: the one that will uproot us, bring us to our knees and force us to experience transformation as rapidly as possible. In the case of boundaries, we will find ourselves in a situation where our boundaries are crossed, broken or become completely invisible. Our self-worth will shrivel away and we will need to confront the behaviour that got us to this point.

For me, that moment was long before I met my husband – when I dated a man with a porn addiction.

If you have ever dated a man with a porn addiction, you will realise that it is a life of broken boundaries, a double life of addictive behaviours. Love dissolves quickly and you are soon living in a constant state of paranoid fear. The sex becomes rough and uncomfortable over time. The sandpaper of two bodies rubbing starts to scratch away your precious heart, erode your self-esteem, your spirit, and nearly all your boundaries disappear. It's a lonely, exhausting journey, one that left me lost and truly broken.

At first, I brushed off the signs, convincing myself that it was just a phase or a harmless habit that every man had. But as time went on, I started to feel the weight of his addiction bearing down on me. More than that, it was consuming me. It was like living in the shadow of an invisible third party, always lurking in the background and whispering doubt into my ear.

I questioned my worth, my attractiveness, my ability to satisfy him. I wondered if I could ever be enough to compete with the fantasy world that he tapped into online daily. I experienced new discoveries and disclosures over and over again, and mistakenly thought it would hurt less with time, that I could look past his indiscretions. And all the while, I struggled to maintain a façade of normalcy, strutting off to my corporate high-flying job, pretending I was strong enough to justify his secret that was now mine. I hid my pain behind a forced smile.

Through it all, I clung to hope, praying that someday he would see the damage his addiction had caused, and choose instead to fight for me; that one day he would wake up and see how worthy I was.

This was never going to happen. Because I could not see how worthy I was.

I also stayed because he said he wanted children with me. When you are childless later in life, and you find someone who wants to have children with you, well, it can feel like you have hit the jackpot. This was the dangling carrot for the biggest boundary breach I ever experienced in my dating life.

I should have run faster than Usain Bolt away from him. The strain of the relationship left a painfully thin, anxious ghost in its wake; not a woman who could mother a child and create a family. Yet I chose to stay. Worse still, I chose to live with him.

Two days after moving in, I developed shingles. My body was screaming out to run in the other direction. We can only betray the feedback that our bodies give us for so long, then our bodies start to betray us.

Months later, I was sitting across from my psychologist, when she asked me pointedly, 'What is your hard boundary, Sheila? What is your walk-away point? When will enough be enough?'

She had been listening to my dysfunctional relationship stories for months now and could see that I still had not grasped that I needed to leave him of my own volition. So, she adopted a new tactic – it was time for hard truths. 'How many times does he have to use porn in a day, before you know your boundary limit has been reached?'

Interesting question, I thought. One that I had never considered. A metric that I could measure. The accountant within me liked her approach. Yet I stumbled, embarrassed that I was even speaking a number out loud. 'Maybe four times,' I replied meekly.

'Four times it is,' she replied matter-of-factly and noted this in her thick notepad.

At this point in our relationship, I had stopped doing workshops, retreats or investing any time in myself. Time away meant there was more time for him to use porn. I had become vigilant, stealthy and spent a lot of time quietly at home, watching.

But after that session with my psychologist, I took a first little step to reclaim my spiritual passions. A week later, I did a weekend workshop with the expert Brian Weiss to study past-life regression. In the workshop, there was a lot of space for contemplation. At one point, I asked my higher self to show me the way forward and to please allow the sign to be very clear.

Asking for a sign from the universe was my next little step. I was becoming ready to listen!

When I got home from the workshop, I was buzzing after connecting with so many like-minded spiritual people, learning a topic that I was passionate about and connecting back to myself. I was inspired to have a romantic night with my man. I spontaneously came out into the living room in some sexy underwear, and as I slowly and seductively walked towards him, he sheepishly said he wasn't in the mood.

And like the lines from a perfect script he said, 'I have already used (porn) four times today. I just can't go again.'

My mouth dropped. That was my metric, my walk-away moment, the boundary I had put down had been crossed. And he had now confirmed this in a way I could not ignore.

A 'hard no' is required when we tolerate experiences that breach our physical, emotional or mental well-being. The examples are endless, and often involve trying to control someone else's behaviour, such as: gaslighting, verbal abuse, infidelity, bullying, belittling. When we need to set boundaries against such experiences, we will often need to seek support, either professionally or with a trusted friend. This is because there are likely to be many blind spots and dysfunctional childhood patterns playing out, and we are unskilled and under-resourced to deal with these 'big stuff' experiences alone.

For me, this included sharing stories of what I was experiencing in my relationship with my friends, with a sense of normalcy that made the severity of the boundary breach obvious to everyone but me. I couldn't see the boundary I needed to set, let alone how to enforce it.

When I did see it, I was ashamed of how long I had tolerated his behaviour. I had allowed drama into my life that was constantly escalating. I had kept his secret. And, worst still, I had enabled his behaviour.

It was time to walk away. It was time to choose me.

But I didn't leave in that moment. I allowed two days for the sediments of clarity to sink in. For 48 hours, I practised compassion for what I had put myself through. Then, I sat down with him and calmly said I was leaving. No drama, no outbursts. He knew I was done. He didn't fight. He knew that our relationship had hit the firm brick wall of a boundary.

There can be calmness when we decide to put a boundary in place and walk away. That calmness may be partly a result of exhaustion and resignation, but it is also the setting of a new foundation of self-respect.

When we are unable to implement a healthy boundary on our own, thus needing external help, we are at least ready to honour the truth of the situation, that things are only getting worse and will not change. When we do this, we arm ourselves with tools, a newfound self-awareness and a glimmer of hope for a better life. We finally feel strong enough to assert our boundaries and stick to them: this is usually through the act of leaving, or a discussion about leaving.

After you enforce your first 'hard no', you will find this is the beginning of many more 'nos' of varying degrees.

The first big boundary breach and how we overcome it is our teacher.

Learning to speak up

'I didn't set this boundary to either please or offend you.
I did it to manage the goals and priorities I have set for my life.'

– DANNY SILK

We often find ourselves caught in a relentless cycle of overwork and self-sacrifice, where boundaries blur and self-care takes a backseat to excessive productivity. When coaching women about workplace boundaries, I have found that women's voices become a whisper; their financial worth becomes a question, not a fact; and they are prepared to shoulder an imbalance in workload to prove themselves in the quest to rise.

We find ourselves navigating a landscape where the demands of our jobs often exceed the capacity of our souls. We push ourselves to the limit, sacrificing our well-being at the altar of productivity and success. And yet, despite our tireless efforts, many of us still find ourselves undervalued and underpaid, our worth measured not by our contributions but by our ability to endure.

In this culture of constant connectivity and 24/7 availability, it's all too easy to lose sight of where work ends and life begins. We check emails late into the night, sacrifice weekends and holidays for the sake of a deadline and measure our worth by our output. In the process, we forget that boundaries are essential for our well-being; they allow us to rest, recharge and reconnect with ourselves and our loved ones.

But we can't be victims here. We can shift our mindset to view setting boundaries as an act of tending to the sacred garden of our souls, a practice that nurtures our mental health and emotional well-being. It's about asserting our rights and ensuring our needs are met, without diminishing the value of others. This is the path to adulthood, to learn how to deal with authority and regulate our nervous systems when we feel threatened.

We may have had experiences in our childhood where we sought to please a parent (or anyone with a strong overbearing personality), and stayed silent to avoid experiencing their anger, rage or disapproval. This pattern then followed us into our adulthood, seeping into our workplaces. But we can change this.

So, where do we start when wanting to put a career and workplace boundary in place?

If boundary setting is new to you, it will feel like tiptoeing through a minefield. The main problem is that, by the time we are of adult age and highly skilled professionally, many of us are grossly under-skilled in the art of having respectful boundary conversations, so under-skilled that we don't even start.

My advice is to address the elephant in the room head-on, whether you want to have this conversation about work or a relationship. Picture this: you're sitting across from your boss or colleague, heart pounding, palms sweaty, nerves frazzled. You take a deep breath and dive right in.

'It's taking some serious courage for me to have this conversation with you today,' you might say. 'I've been putting it off because I've been nervous about how you'll respond. But speaking up means a lot to me, so here goes: Can I share some concerns I've been grappling with lately?'

Taking this little step of owning your truth like that is a game-changer. It sets the tone for open, honest communication and lays the groundwork for building healthy boundaries that honour both you and your colleagues.

> Little Brave Acts *are commonly conversations*
> *with those we fear judgment from the most.*

In my years of coaching corporate women, I have witnessed the powerful truth that when they engage in the *Little Brave Act* of speaking up, they don't have any repeated childhood experiences of anger, punishment, belittling or embarrassment. Quite the opposite really. Most of the time, they are met with an adult response that sounds something like, 'I didn't know you were experiencing these challenges; how can I help? I don't want to see you upset like this.'

The *Little Brave Act* of speaking up will require a ton of courage, as it may be the first time you are talking about your pay, work hours, how someone is treating you at work or even your dissatisfaction about the type of work you are doing. When we start empowering ourselves with the brave act of a conversation, we can be surprised when we are met with empathy, rapport and compassion – but this is the reward of bravery.

Brave conversations

'When we fail to set boundaries and hold people
accountable, we feel used and mistreated.'

– BRENÉ BROWN

I have seen many women stumble and falter when it comes to having brave conversations. It's like there's a knot in our throats, a heaviness in our chests, as we struggle to voice our needs and our desires. We become tongue-tied and mute when it comes to seemingly simple statements, as we grapple with the fear of being seen as weak, needy or demanding:

'I can't work late tonight.'

'I need to work from home today, my child is sick.'

'I'd like to discuss my salary.'

'I am feeling overwhelmed by my workload.'

Statements such as these are not signs of weakness – they're signs of strength. They're a cry for help, a request for support, an acknowldgment of difficulty. They are also an acknowledgment of our self-worth. And yet, too often, we silence ourselves; we martyr ourselves – all while anger and resentment bubble beneath the surface.

The *Little Brave Act* of having the conversation that's needed is the first critical little step to establishing a healthy boundary, and this applies to non-work conversations as well. It applies to conversations about sexual preferences, domestic workloads, friendship boundaries, etc.

So, let's talk about the different types of conversations we tend to have – or not have.

First, there are the conversations we *do have* – or rather, the ones we think we're having. These are the ones where we dance around our truth, where we apologise for making a request, or where we hold back out of fear of rocking the boat. Needless to say, these conversations rarely lead to the outcomes we desire.

Then there are the conversations that *play out* in our heads – the ones where we imagine ourselves as the hero; our boss, partner or friend as the villain; and our words as weapons. In these scenarios, we're the true victor, unleashing a torrent of unspoken truths and demands. But let's be real: these conversations rarely see the light of day, and even if they do, they usually end in disaster.

And finally, there are the conversations *we wish* we could have – the ones where we show up as our adult selves, speaking our truth with courage and conviction. These are the conversations that embrace vulnerability, that invite connection, that pave the way for growth and understanding. These are also the conversations where we risk disappointing another person. Can we strive for more of these conversations – the ones that move us forward, that strengthen our relationships, that honour the truth of who we are? Because when we dare to speak our truth, we open the door to possibility, to growth, to true connection. And that is where the magic happens.

Boundaries aren't just about saying no; they're
also about saying yes to what truly matters.

Glennon Doyle in her book, *Untamed*, writes, 'Every time you're given a choice between disappointing someone else and disappointing yourself, your duty is to disappoint that someone else. Your job, throughout your entire life, is to disappoint as many people as it takes to avoid disappointing yourself.' I love the sentiment in this statement. We need this type of brave mindset when we are *initially* implementing boundaries.

As we learn to speak up – whether it's at work or in our relationships – we're essentially flexing a muscle. It's a muscle that grows stronger with each brave conversation, each step we take towards engaging in more adult and balanced dialogue.

However, I have found that we don't need to experience an *outcome* of disappointing another. When we become better at putting boundaries in place, we start to realise something powerful: the person we're conversing with might actually be reasonable. They might be open to hearing us out, to being flexible, to finding common ground. It's a revelation, really –

an acknowledgment that we're not alone in this, that there's potential for understanding and compromise on both sides.

As we navigate these conversations, we also learn the art of negotiation. We discover how to dance back and forth, how to find that delicate balance where both parties feel heard, understood and respected. It's a skill that takes practice, patience, and yes, many repetitions.

Now, there is a misconception that speaking up at work can be career limiting. But I have found it to be quite the opposite – career expanding, in fact – as it demonstrates maturity, a clarity of your personal vision, and that you know how to take care of yourself. It's like you're waving a flag that says, 'Hey, world, I know who I am, I know what I need, and I'm not afraid to ask for it.'

I remember back when I was a chief finance officer, interviewing candidate after candidate for a key role. You know what question I always made sure to ask? It wasn't about their technical skills or their past experience. No, it was about their ability to set boundaries, to take care of themselves in the high-stakes corporate world. Because in those roles, where the pressure is high and the stakes are even higher, you need to know how to stand your ground. You need to know how to protect your energy, your sanity, your well-being. Those who could demonstrate that they knew how to take care of themselves autonomously were the ones I knew would thrive, succeed and go the distance.

Let's debunk that myth once and for all: speaking up isn't career-limiting – it's career-igniting. It's the secret sauce that sets you apart, propels you forward and paves the way for long-term success.

Speak your truth, set those boundaries and watch as your career skyrockets to new heights.

The dance of rupture and repair

*'Boundaries are the distance at which I can
love you and me simultaneously.'*

– PRENTIS HEMPHILL

Boundary setting can also be about preserving and expanding the love between two people. Long, enduring friendships that start in high school or university, or span decades, will inevitably need to navigate transitions in life. Each of us moves through the seasons of life at our own pace, in our own way. Thus, learning how to set boundaries is crucial for not only the longevity of a friendship, but to also see the friendship thrive and grow.

Planning to have a child brought to the surface a new boundary conversation for me with my dearest friend. It caught me off guard, as I believed we had laid the groundwork for boundaries years earlier in our 25-year friendship. Yet, here we were, navigating the shifting tides of change together.

After her 50th birthday celebrations, we were reflecting on milestone events and giggling like we were 20-year-olds. But beneath the surface of our joy, a wave of anxiety washed over me as I confided in Darlean about my concerns of running my business and being a mother at the same time.

Mid-sentence, I noticed a subtle shift in Darlean's expression – the slight crinkle of her nose, the flicker of disapproval in her eyes. Years of friendship had honed my ability to read her unspoken language, and I knew she wasn't on board with what I was proposing. She blurted out, 'They are babies for such a short time; are you sure that's what you want to do?'

I could feel the weight of her words and the mother guilt within me begin to bubble to the surface. My immediate response was to shut down. My instinctive response was to retreat into myself, my words becoming guarded, my tone defensive, my manner cautious. The space between us suddenly felt unsafe for both of us.

Darlean instinctively knew it was time to leave, which really meant escape. 'I have a lot of work to get done today, I need to go.'

I jumped to my feet and opened the door for her quickly. Her departure was a mutual agreement, an unspoken acknowledgment that we both needed space to process our emotions, to retreat into the solitude of our own thoughts. With a hurried goodbye, she slipped out the door, leaving a lingering sense of unease in her wake. We were experiencing a rupture in our relationship.

A rupture in a relationship is a break in the connection between two people. It often signals a breakdown in boundaries, where the once-clear lines of respect and understanding blur, leaving both parties vulnerable to a storm of misunderstanding and discord. Ruptures are a normal part of all relationships. Sadly, when repeated ruptures occur without any repair, it can feel like walls can build up between people over time. Love gets replaced by resentment, causing a relationship to erode.

Often such ruptures stem from clashes of values – fundamental differences in the way we choose to live our lives and express ourselves. In recent times, such conflicts have surfaced in discussions surrounding vaccinations, politics, family values, foreign wars and child-rearing practices. As topics like these become more polarised, the potential for ruptures in relationships grows, highlighting the importance of communication, empathy and mutual respect in bridging our divides and preserving the bonds that unite us.

When the dynamics shift in a loving relationship, it's natural to feel uncertain about where new boundaries lie. In that uncertainty, we might find ourselves allowing others to make decisions for us, convincing ourselves that we're just 'going with the flow'. But deep down, this is often rooted in a fear of losing the relationship – the love, safety and comfort it provides.

If left unacknowledged, the relationship will, over time, cease to be safe and supportive.

Darlean and I could have easily brushed off our uncomfortable conversation, hoping that time would sweep it under the rug and allow us to move forward, as if nothing had happened. But that would have been a disservice to us and to our relationship. So we had to take a little step.

The *Little Brave Act* of acknowledging any discomfort, then addressing the underlying issues and establishing clear boundaries, can nurture and protect the bonds that matter most to us. It's not always easy to step into such acts, as it requires vulnerability and courage. But in the end, it's the only way to ensure that our relationships remain safe, supportive and true to who we are.

Dr John Demartini breaks down relationships into three distinct categories: careful, careless and caring.

In *careful* relationships, we feel compelled to adopt the values of the other person, neglecting our own needs and desires in the process. This often leads to a constant state of walking on eggshells, tiptoeing around to avoid conflict or disappointment.

On the other hand, in *careless* relationships, we project our own values onto others, oblivious to theirs. It's like we're wearing blinders, only seeing our own perspective and disregarding theirs entirely.

Neither of these approaches are sustainable in the long run and inevitably lead to the relationship's breakdown.

But then there's the *caring* relationship – the holy grail, if you will. In a caring relationship, we not only communicate our own values but also take time to understand and respect the values of the other person, even when they differ from our own. It's a delicate dance of mutual consideration and appreciation, where both sides feel honoured and respected.

In a caring relationship, there's no need to tiptoe or project – instead, there's open communication, empathy, and a genuine desire to understand and support each other. It's a beautiful balance that nurtures the relationship and allows it to flourish over time.

The days without communication between Darlean and me felt like an eternity, the silence echoing loudly in my mind, a constant reminder of the rupture in our friendship. But then, a week later, a text from her appeared on my phone – a gentle reminder that even in the midst of conflict, love still remained. Her words, though simple, held immense power.

'I just wanted to make sure you were feeling okay after our conversation ...'

It was a lifeline thrown into the waters of uncertainty, a testament to the depth of our friendship and the strength of our bond.

In that moment, a wave of relief washed over me. Darlean wasn't just reaching out to check on my well-being; she was extending an olive branch, offering a path back to connection and understanding. And with her next words of reassurance, I felt seen, heard and valued in a way that only true friends can make you feel: 'I know you always know the right thing to do for you.'

We had danced this dance of rupture and repair many times before, navigating the twists and turns of our relationship with grace and resilience. We knew that repair was essential to nurturing our love and respect, to ensuring the longevity of our friendship. When Darlean took that brave step forward to text me, acknowledging our differences and extending the hand of reconciliation, my heart swelled with love and gratitude. It was a *Little Brave Act* for her, a testament to the depth of her character and the strength of our bond; and in that moment, I loved her more than ever before.

Boundaries are a love language.

Through the dance of rupture and repair, we can discover that our differences are not barriers. With each *Little Brave Act* in our loving relationships, our love can grow deeper, our bonds stronger and our friendships more resilient than ever before.

Finding our inner boundaries

*'Sometimes the easiest way to solve a problem
is to stop participating in the problem.'*

– JONATHAN MEAD

We all love a good drama. It's why reality TV shows, soap operas and gossip columns are so addictive. But in real life, drama can be toxic and downright exhausting.

When we face major life transitions, our skill in boundary setting is tested. This is particularly the case when the structure of our families change and we have to set strong inner boundaries about what we will and won't accept. If we don't, we are setting ourselves up for a life of drama and conflict.

With half of all marriages ending in divorce, combined with people living longer, having multiple partners and blending families like never before, it's clear that navigating the chaos of break-ups is a crucial skill. We need to learn how to step out of the drama of divorce and separation. It's not just important – it's essential. It's about learning to rise above the chaos, finding peace in the midst of change, and embracing the messy, glorious, brave life that comes next.

The types of drama seen in divorce are utterly heartbreaking and seemingly endless. Communication in particular, or rather the lack of it, becomes a daily exercise in frustration. Every text and email is a potential landmine. Custody battles turn every conversation into a showdown, where everyone is convinced they are the better parent. The kids are stuck in the middle, trying to make sense of their new reality. Then there's the financial drama – child support and who pays for what can make you feel like you're starring in a never-ending episode of *Judge Judy*. Parenting styles clash spectacularly. Extended family members, each with their own opinions and advice, add to the chaos.

Sally thought her divorce would be different, a textbook case of consciously uncoupling from her husband. In fact, she and her husband even shared a laugh when he signed the divorce papers. Picture this: they were in the lawyer's office, and there was only one chair. So, he ends up kneeling against the table to sign the papers. When their lawyer offered him a chair, he quipped, 'This is the last time I will be getting down on one knee.' They had been consciously uncoupled for two years by then. Their nine-year-old son even remarked at lunch, 'I think it is better that you are separated, Mum; you seem happier.'

Fast forward two years. Robert was back down on one knee and there is an impending wedding – to Nina. From this point, drama entered Sally's life.

Sally now found herself embroiled in constant conflicts with the new wife. Every interaction felt like a battle, every co-parenting decision turned into a war. Sally, Nina and Robert were stuck in a drama triangle.

The *drama triangle* is the brainchild of psychologist Dr Stephen Karpman. He was passionate about psychology, and also acting. He knew that any movie worth watching had an incredible amount of drama in it, and that the characters played certain roles to create this drama. He understood that just as in the movies, we play certain roles in real life that create similar types of drama in ways that do not serve us.

In the drama triangle there are three roles: the victim, the rescuer and the persecutor. Any one of us can play any of these roles, depending on the circumstances.

The victim is the part of us that feels powerless and overwhelmed by life. It's the voice that says, 'I can't do this; it's too much.' This role keeps us stuck in a place of helplessness, waiting for someone to come and save us.

Then there's the rescuer. This role feels most alive when it's saving others, believing that their worth is tied to being needed. Rescuers often sacrifice their own well-being, thinking they're helping; but in reality, they prevent others from growing and finding their strength.

Lastly, we have the persecutor. This role emerges from our own pain and fear, projecting blame and criticism onto others to feel a false sense of control. Persecutors create conflict and hurt, masking their vulnerability.

Sally, Nina and Robert were playing the roles of victim and persecutor, each swapping roles depending on the circumstance. The rescuers were family and friends and, uncomfortably for them, their son. It was a never-ending cycle of blame, guilt and resentment.

I started working with Sally to support her through this major life transition, and also to help bring awareness of the role she was playing in the drama and to empower her to move away from it. But the problem was that Sally lacked boundaries and self-love.

Her lack of boundaries meant that she came to each session feeling more and more wronged, disempowered and disillusioned. Sally shared the heartache of missing out on Mother's Day because her son was with his new stepmother, Nina. This felt like the sting of a thousand paper cuts. Major holidays became strategic negotiations. Battling over who got to attend school concerts turned into a tug-of-war, with each side trying to claim the moral high ground. Her ex-husband's side of the family – with their big, boisterous gatherings – made her small, quiet clan feel even more isolated. And when it came to their son's birthday, giving gifts early because the big day was with his dad's new family made her feel like she was always a step behind. Through it all, she was trying to maintain her sanity and grace, keeping her child's best interests at heart while navigating the emotional minefield that was her new reality.

Things came to a head when Sally was out for lunch with her son one day. Forty minutes into the lunch, he casually dropped into the conversation, 'And by the way, Mum, I am changing schools. The new school needs your approval tomorrow.'

Sally shared, 'I was shocked, speechless, angry. Then I suddenly felt helpless and numb.' She later found out that this decision had been made many weeks prior; her son had already bought his new school uniform. Sally had not been included in this major decision, one made by Robert and his new wife.

As Sally and I reflected in a session, she had let too many boundary breaches go, silencing herself, over compromising, not wanting to 'rock the boat' too much, all the while trying to walk the higher ground.

But now Sally was tired of the drama. She was sick of the emotional whiplash and knew she had to make major changes. Sally realised that the only way to step out of the drama triangle was to set firm, healthy boundaries. This wasn't about controlling others but about protecting her own peace.

Her work was deep and challenging at times. She had to unpack the drama in her home as a child, drama that she had unconsciously become use to, and she reflected on the fears she had had as a little girl to please her mother. She realised that the dysfunction in her parents' marriage had found a mirror in her own marriage and other relationships.

Sally also gained the self-awareness that she, her ex-husband and his new wife had been playing all three roles in the drama triangle – victim, rescuer and persecutor. It was a moment of painful clarity, realising that she'd been stuck in a loop of her own making. But this awareness was the key to her freedom.

We quite often play multiple roles in life, and we can stop playing any one of those roles simply by establishing boundaries. The outcome of choosing to establish boundaries and stop playing a drama triangle role, is that we see a reduction in the drama in our lives.

With this new awareness, Sally stepped out of the drama triangle and took her life back. She stopped seeing herself as a pawn in someone else's game and started owning her life. She set boundaries that protected her peace. She learned to sit with her discomfort instead of rescuing others from theirs. She stopped blaming and started healing. No longer trapped in the endless cycle of drama, this is where her real transformation could begin.

Sounds like an easy quick fix? Not quite. Initially her ongoing interactions with Nina were like an intense game of ping-pong – quick back-and-forth exchanges, constantly navigating those boundary lines, each of them trying to score a point, fair and square. It wasn't always smooth, but it was real, and it was necessary.

Life still threw challenges her way, but Sally faced them with a renewed sense of strength and clarity. She learned that the only way to truly win is to stop playing the game. And that, my friends, is how you break free from the drama triangle.

Is this always easy? No! The reality of divorce is that difficult conversations and dynamics will always be a part of the picture, and we'll find ourselves getting triggered.

When this happens to Sally, she regulates herself. She feels the emotions rising in her body, listens to what her body is telling her, and trusts that a trigger has occurred. Then, she places her hand on her heart and pours all her raw emotions into her journal. These are the five questions she asks herself every time she is triggered:

What is it that I am feeling?

Where am I feeling it?

What triggered it?

What am I making it mean?

If this isn't the case, how else can I look at the situation?

The *Little Brave Act* of asking and answering these questions, reduces the drama internally, and thus externally. This is her way of reclaiming peace. From that space, we are then more resourced to respond.

Sally's next little step was to ask herself: 'How can I be compassionate for myself and have compassion for Nina at the same time?'

Why is this important to address? Drama drains our energy and keeps us from living authentically. Reducing drama is like cleaning out our email inbox – it's necessary and liberating. Without the constant soap opera of stress, we can actually focus on our mental and emotional health; our relationships get better too, and we become more productive, making decisions with the clarity of a Zen master. When we ditch the drama, we create space for personal growth, peace and a lot more joy – and who doesn't want a life filled with more joy and less chaos?

Over the year that followed, Sally gained confidence in clearly communicating her needs and limits. She stopped engaging in petty arguments and refused to be drawn into unnecessary conflicts. She also embraced self-love. She focused on her own well-being, nurturing her physical, emotional and mental health. She began to see herself not as a victim but as the hero of her own story.

To leave drama behind, we have to rewrite the narrative. Victims need to take control and start creating solutions. Rescuers need to stop fixing and start coaching others to handle their own problems. Persecutors need to switch from blaming to challenging others constructively. It's all about setting boundaries and taking responsibility. When you do this, you step out of the drama and start living a more empowered and authentic life.

Boundaries are not about keeping others out; they are about keeping ourselves in – keeping ourselves aligned with our vision and committed to our path. They are a declaration of our self-worth, protecting our energy and time, while allowing us to thrive authentically. They allow us to prioritise what truly matters, to say no to what doesn't serve us and to create a life that reflects our most authentic aspirations. The *Little Brave Act* of setting your boundaries will create the foundation of a life that honours ourselves and the dreams we are bravely bringing to life.

Brave truths

- It's okay to feel discomfort or guilt when setting boundaries. Remember, discomfort is the price of admission to a meaningful life.

- Boundaries aren't just about saying no: they're also about saying yes to what truly matters. It is an act of self-care and self-respect.

- Boundaries are a love language. They are the backbone of healthy relationships. They ensure that our connections are rooted in mutual respect and understanding.

- For boundaries to be effective, we must communicate them clearly and confidently. *Little Brave Acts* are commonly conversations with those who we fear judgment from the most.

- By setting boundaries, you prevent yourself from being pulled into the toxic dynamics of the drama triangle.

Brave questions

- What fears are holding you back from setting boundaries, and how can you face those fears with bravery and self-compassion?

- What areas of your life feel most draining right now, and what boundaries can you set to protect your energy?

- Who in your life consistently oversteps your boundaries, and how can you clearly communicate your needs to them?

- What past experiences have taught you about the importance of boundaries, and how can you use those lessons to guide you now?

- Why do you feel you always need to be 'on' 24/7? What positive change would happen in your life if you weren't on 24/7?

Brave mantra

With every *Little Brave Act*, I set boundaries that honour my vision.

CHAPTER 9

The powerful little step of blooming late

'I'm late, I'm late, for a very important date!
No time to say "Hello, Good Bye" I'm late, I'm late, I'm late!'

—WHITE RABBIT, *ALICE IN WONDERLAND*

Haven't accomplished all your dreams yet? Feeling like time is slipping away while your plans seem to flail and falter? Don't panic — maybe you're a late bloomer! Being a late bloomer means your journey is uniquely yours, unfolding in its perfect time. Remember, Plan A and Plan B have to fail for you to discover the brilliance of Plan C. And this will inevitably happen later than you expect and definitely not on your timeline.

A late bloomer is a person who honours their own divine timing, refusing to be rushed by the ticking clocks in a world obsessed with early accomplishment. They understand that true transformation requires patience and pressure, like diamonds forming deep within the earth. They embrace the deep burrowing, the rich rooting, knowing that their moment to bloom will come when they are ready to unfurl their fullest, most radiant selves. Their journey is a testament to the power of timing and trust in one's own unique rhythm.

Embracing lateness

'You can start late, look different, be uncertain, and still succeed.'

– MISTY COPELAND

Given how easily our traditional plans can tempt and distract us with the promise of belonging, acceptance and success, we must forgive ourselves for initially devoting so much time and energy in the pursuit of our Plan As and Bs. Life with its predictable unpredictability means that these plans may fail in the middle of our life, or later. And we are left running late. We may find ourselves financially ruined, single, without a career, parenting on our own. All of this requires us to start over. It takes time to heal, time to reflect and grow, time to map out another more authentic path forward. And as a result, we bloom late.

Still, it's easy to feel disappointed with the timing of certain aspects of our lives – whether we have children early, then become a mature-aged student and embark on a career later; or we have a career earlier and delay motherhood, which was how my life has unravelled; or we marry early but really only understand true soulmate love when walking down the aisle to husband number two or three.

It's important to remember that we *all* feel late at some point in our lives. How could we not? We live in a world where there are multiple milestones expected at almost every age!

Not that there is *anyone* watching or grading us on how quickly we achieve our dreams. Why not embrace the 'lateness' in your life, wherever it arises?

It's never too late for a Little Brave Act.

Just as a part of you will know as you transition through change that you *are* on time, that your life path *is* unfolding, that you *can* allow your identity to take shape quietly and at your own pace in the process of healing and self-discovery. You may resist this at times, as the judgment for being late can feel overwhelming, and shame can arise. At the same time, the old soul within you *knows* that there is no expiration to your personal evolution. For late bloomers, there is much healing to do, and healing cannot be rushed.

There is a quiet power in waiting.

I am a proud late bloomer. I started my second career, my true calling, in my 40s. I married at the age of 45. And as for becoming a mother, well, that would unfold over time. For these big Ms, 'married' and 'mother', by societal standards I was late. Yet my little step was to accept that arriving where we need to be was always meant to happen later in life. I challenged the notion of being 'late' and what is 'on time' – constructs that completely ignored my mental mindset, my physical abilities or when my gifts surfaced.

To know that we are late bloomers, and to accept this about ourselves, may be the most radical and powerful act of self-love that we can make as a woman.

A lesson from nature

'Extraordinary accomplishments come from doing ordinary things for extraordinary periods of time.'

– ALEX HORMOZI

I first heard about the agave plant on a nature tour in Sedona, Arizona. My husband and I had just completed seven rounds of IVF and we needed a holiday, a break from trying to push forward with a plan that was no longer working. We were on a jeep tour when our tour guide remarked, 'Did you know that the agave plant only blooms once and this bloom tends to happen at the end of its long life?'

I reflected on how patient the residents to this region must be to wait for this blooming, and how it must be celebrated when it does occur. I also wondered why this tree only flowered once, at the end of its life.

The agave's single awe-inspiring bloom, characterised by vibrant hues and intricate patterns, speaks to the significance of moments in our lives, emphasising the importance of waiting for the right time to fully embrace and showcase our capabilities. In a world that often demands instant results, the agave's patient growth reminds us that meaningful accomplishments often require time and dedication.

Side hustles that are sustainable take time – those late nights, testing and tweaking. Marriages built on strong foundations take time – constantly recommitting with deep, soul-stretching conversations. Careers take time – years of showing up and performing. Legacy wealth takes time – with smart strategic moves and sacrifices. And fertility journeys can take longer than expected – navigating hopes and heartbreaks. Patience isn't just a virtue – it's a necessity.

Your full blossoming will happen. It may just take time.

Much like the agave, which takes years to reach maturity before gracing the world with its magnificent flower spike, we often find ourselves on a prolonged journey towards personal and professional fulfilment.

Jan's powerful little step: blooming late

'Life really does begin at forty.
Up until then, you are just doing research.'

– CARL JUNG

Late bloomers often find their true calling when others are settling into their comfort zones. There is a liberation in the process of self-discovery and embracing who we are. Quite often this takes time, sometimes many years.

Take my client Jan, for example. She had just won a bodybuilding competition and was confidently strutting across the stage to collect her trophy. She was rocking a pair of hooker-high heels, sporting a radioactive orange tan from head to toe, and flashing a set of blinding white teeth. She was radiating an infectious confidence as she strategically flexed her muscles. But the best part? She was feeling absolutely fabulous. As she scanned the cheering crowd, she realised she was visible, relevant, and – just like that – she found her true purpose.

Jan was 63.

The physical journey for ageing women is often riddled with challenges – invisibility when you're over 40, irrelevancy when you're over 50, and ignored when you're over 60. Just as we might begin to embrace the empowerment of wisdom born from years of living, new societal or technological challenges emerge. At this point we must confront our limiting beliefs, challenge any unhealthy collective views, and rewrite our own narratives. If we don't, we will become a victim to those beliefs. Worse than that, we may even perpetuate them.

Of course, challenging beliefs and rewriting our narratives is not easy. It will demand much from us, stretching our hearts and minds in ways we never imagined. Quite often there is no template handed to us from our mothers or older women. We are pioneers.

'I never wanted to be a bodybuilder,' Jan shared with me. 'When I was 40, my world shattered. My husband cheated on me and I was devastated. I quickly moved in with a friend who happened to be a personal trainer. She saw potential in me that I couldn't see in myself. She believed my body would respond beautifully to weight training and that it could be a powerful outlet for my anger and frustration. Living with her meant I couldn't quit – she was always there, holding me accountable, helping me transform my pain into strength.'

'It was twelve weeks of total mind and body transformation. It is life-changing to put yourself through such a regime. It not only strengthens your muscles but also your mind.' Starting this training was one of Jan's first little steps.

She then entered her first bodybuilding competition, her next *Little Brave Act*.

'I never entered to win, just to better myself. I was so scared. I borrowed someone else's bikini. This was 25 years ago now! I had to find a way to love myself. It was so clichéd – my husband cheating on me when I reached my 40s! I knew it had been going on for a long time. But I stayed. It was time for me to love myself.'

Jan was learning the lesson of visibility.

At 50, Jan then entered her second bodybuilding competition. This was just after the global financial crisis of 2007–09, and her career had now collapsed. She was fighting to find relevance in a field of recruitment that demanded youthful vitality, stamina and drive.

'I knew that entering another bodybuilding competition would help me with my mental strength. I had already done a lot of work on my self-esteem by this time in my life. I needed the *mental* strength to reinvent myself.'

A few years after that, Jan's mother became very ill.

'I felt called to return home to take care of my mother.'

In this, Jan was learning the lesson of relevance. The role of taking care of our ageing and ill parents is never a part of our life plan. Yet, we can reset our mindset to see the healing and transformation that this process can provide us.

'It was such an important time with my mother. Looking back, I am so grateful for the healing that it provided, as I was always the black sheep of the family. My mother finally got to know me for me, and so did my siblings. I couldn't run away. I had been running for most of my life.'

I started mentoring Jan when she was in her late 50s. I have always had a fascination with bodybuilding and bodybuilders, since I was a child. I'm not sure if I am in awe of them for the discipline and mental strength needed to compete, or if I find myself intrigued at the pomp and show displayed. Regardless, I was impressed with Jan's personal accomplishments. I knew that if I found Jan inspiring, then many around the world would do so too. So, in a mentoring session, I suggested that she finish her Certificate 3 in Fitness and start training women like herself. I also wanted her to start sharing on social media to women her age, about how she stayed fit, healthy and vibrant. There were so many people who needed her wisdom and knowledge!

Just 12 weeks later, Jan had 45,000 new followers on Instagram. Jan's *Little Brave Act* of sharing her story on social media meant that she was rewriting the script of what it meant to age with grace, wisdom and unapologetic authenticity. She had cultivated the inner wisdom and acquired the knowledge to heal and empower herself, and eventually help thousands of women. This was never something she had planned to do.

One year later, she entered her third bodybuilding competition. Much like the agave plant, she finally came into full bloom – winning the competition in her early 60s.

But unlike the agave, this is not her final bloom. After winning the competition, Jan started Ageless Transformations, where she inspires, motivates and teaches women (and men) over the age of 50 how to embrace change, be visible, find relevance and resurrect their goals, especially at a time in life when it can feel overwhelming and impossible.

The American journalist and author Rich Karlgaard has insightfully described the journey of late bloomers as follows: 'They fulfill their potential frequently in novel and unexpected ways, surprising even those closest to them. They are not attempting to satisfy, with gritted teeth, the expectations of their parents or society, a false path that leads to burnout and brittleness, or even to depression and illness. Late bloomers are those who find their supreme destiny on their own schedule, in their own way.'

I couldn't agree more!

It took three bodybuilding competitions over three decades for Jan's purpose, wisdom and experience to come to fruition. This is what late blooming looks like. It was worth the wait.

Is there a deadline for finding your soulmate?

'Timing is everything. No matter how old you are, finding the guy who's in the same place as you and wants to show up is the only way a relationship works, period.'

– CAMERON DIAZ

When I was 21, I went to see a psychic. I drove over an hour to her home, fuelled by a mix of curiosity and desperation. Her husband answered the door and gave me that knowing look, the kind that says, 'Ah, another lost spiritual soul seeking answers from the void.' He pointed to the back room, and I found myself pushing through a hanging wall of beads into a mysterious, dimly lit room filled with the thick aroma of incense smoke. I sat down, took a deep breath, and asked the question most psychics get asked: 'When will I meet my soulmate?'

A raven-haired woman in her 50s stared into her crystal ball (yes, she actually had a crystal ball), sighed and looked away. Intuitively, I knew she didn't like what she saw and was hesitant to speak.

'You will marry in your late 40s,' she said eventually. 'Many things will happen for you later in life. You have a lot of healing to do.'

My mouth dropped open and it felt like I had been punched in the gut. She might as well have said that I would be meeting him at 100! Anger immediately rose from a dark, knowing place within me. I hadn't liked what she said, and I didn't want to believe her. 'You have it wrong!' I angrily blurted out.

You see, my Plan A had involved meeting Mr Right at 28 and having three children before the age of 35. No one could tell me otherwise.

This was the plan!!!

Of course, I felt very differently 25 years later, walking down the aisle giddy with excitement and nervousness, yet also grounded and calm. I had spent so long since that psychic reading searching for Tyson, whom I married at the age of 45. The psychic had been right all along. It was written in the stars, this uncomfortable truth: you have a lot of healing to do. And heal I did.

Although, it wasn't until the middle of a Covid lockdown that I found myself ready and able to fully heal.

Many of us responded to Covid with small and big changes. One particular response to the pandemic was to start making significant shifts in our lifestyles because many of us had our priorities out of balance. Slowing down became a gift, a chance to reset. After all, we all become either victims or victors of the choices that we make.

As for me, I was lonely. I was constantly looking into Zoom rooms full of people, families, couples and even family pets – all living in messy houses full of noise and life. Meanwhile, my Zoom background was always the same: neat, orderly, solitary, quiet. Desperately single. I was surrounded by silence and stillness, while everyone else seemed to be living in a whirlwind of connection and chaos. It was a stark reflection of my reality. I realised I needed to change this, quickly and intentionally.

I had been single and lonely before, but this time was different – I used *all* the tools I was teaching my clients and did the big inner work. I wrote a clear list of all the things that I wanted in my partner, and then I stepped into the mindset of being brave. I critically analysed where *I* felt short of that list. I spent months focusing on inner child and trauma work. I owned up to every failed relationship, and I was committed to the process regardless of how uncomfortable it became. Lockdown provided a key to unlock and heal my broken heart, when previously I had been too busy to do such deep work.

Embracing the possibility of transformation through healing at any age, is a *Little Brave Act*. But late bloomers can at least bring their accumulation of experience and wisdom over time to their journey. At the time of blooming, they realise their dreams were always meant to come to fruition later in life.

We have been conditioned with an untruth, that if we haven't done something by a certain age, then it can't be done: healing our trauma, falling pregnant, meeting our soulmate, buying property, backpacking solo around the world, starting a degree. But we can find the strength and resilience to reach our goals at any age. So, when someone says to you it's too late in life for something, what they are really saying is that it's too late for them. Don't listen! It's never too late to live your truth.

A second bloom

'The best time to plant a tree was 20 years ago.
The second-best time is now.'

– CHINESE PROVERB

We often tell ourselves that our prime years are behind us, that the best has come and gone. But what if we rewrote that narrative? What if we dared to believe that our greatest moments are still ahead? Can we bloom more than once in this lifetime? Can the bell curve of our lives have not just one, but two peaks? And perhaps most dauntingly, how do we navigate this second blooming, especially when it occurs in our late 30s, 40s or 50s – a time when the roadmap and support seem scarce? What if we trusted that our most vibrant, powerful selves are yet to come?

To step into the unexpected path, we need to believe that we can bloom twice in our lives. More importantly, we need to take those little steps to facilitate the second bloom.

Eleanor Mills is a pretty big deal. She's interviewed everyone from Mikhail Gorbachev to Sheryl Sandberg to Theresa May. As the editorial director of *The Sunday Times* in the UK she was supposedly at the top of her game. Then, in March 2020, after 22 years at *The Times*, Eleanor was made redundant.

I met Eleanor in May 2020, right in the middle of her life crisis. She looked downtrodden and lost, like so many of us when the rug is pulled out from under our feet.

Eleanor describes the aftermath of the redundancy: 'I was too sad. Too ashamed. Humiliated. Lost. It sounds mad now, but I felt like I had died. There was the same finality. No way back to what my life had been. It was over. Gone. It happened with dizzying speed.' During that initial meeting, we shared our mutual struggles with rebuilding self-esteem after giving so much to our careers. For me, it had cost me a family and a loving partner. We had both lost our connection to ourselves.

While Eleanor had lost her job, she hadn't lost her curiosity, her award-winning journalist skills or her uncanny ability to influence the next zeitgeist. She shifted from interviewing international leaders to connecting with her tribe of women in their 40s and 50s, who were facing similar challenges. Eleanor wanted to understand their struggles and be part of the solution. She aimed to recalibrate how the media and society viewed women in midlife. More importantly, she wanted to reframe how these women saw themselves.

Eleanor and I reconnected six months later, and a lot had changed for her. She was now armed with data, anecdotes and a renewed mission. She shared with me some important insights from her research, 'By the time we reach 50, over half of women have been through at least five big life challenges, including: divorce, bereavement, redundancy, abuse, bankruptcy, illness, coping with tricky teenagers, or elderly parents falling ill and dying.' It is comforting to know that for most, the second blooming will tend to occur after multiple crises.

How do we navigate a second bloom in our lives? First, we must allow our Plan As and Plan Bs to crumble. Next, understand that what got us here won't take us to the next chapter. This happens to everyone at a certain age. We may need to process rage at the world, our bodies and our lives. Grieving, cocooning, revisiting our vision, and loving ourselves are essential parts of this process. This is how we transform and bloom again.

Eleanor's research also shows that, 'Those who have been through and survived the most, are ultimately the happiest. The midlife collision can derail us, but it also clears the way for new beginnings. There's so much happiness on the other side.' This insight helps us step towards our Plan C later in life. It highlights the importance of our *Little Brave Acts* as we embrace our second bloom.

> *Midlife is not an end, but a fertile ground*
> *for our second bloom to flourish.*

Eleanor used her influence, her accumulated wisdom and connections from her first bloom as the editorial director of *The Sunday Times* to help her with her second bloom. She is now the CEO and founder of the media platform noon.org. uk – a community for women pivoting in midlife. She started gathering stories to inspire other women not to give up. And now her bestselling book, *Much More to Come*, has become a beacon for those navigating the complexities of reinvention.

She shared, 'I've always loved the phrase, "You can't be what you can't see." I wanted other women who felt lost and on the scrap heap in midlife to look at Noon and read my story and know that they weren't done. It wasn't over. There was a path to reinvention and another amazing act in life to follow. That there is a positive answer to that dreaded question: what next?'

Noon advocates for a second bloom in life.

You will have multiple blooms in your lifetime. Your job is to bounce back after each setback and find a new purpose and discover the next version of yourself.

Eleanor asked herself these important questions – questions she reflects that had been delayed for too long:

What new passions or interests have I discovered during or after my midlife crisis?

In what ways have I become stronger or more resilient through my midlife challenges?

What aspects of my life bring me the most joy and fulfilment now?

What new goals or dreams am I excited to pursue in this next chapter?

Eleanor shares, 'I am so grateful for what I have been through. I think 50 is the age when we finally become the women we always wanted to be. That is certainly how I have felt.

Life offers us a second bloom, a chance to rediscover our passions and purpose after midlife.

Can we bravely see that life is not a single bloom but a tapestry of seasons, each one more breathtaking than the last. And as you embrace this second bloom with all the grace and grit you can muster, you realise that the best – yes, the very best – is yet to come.

Brave truths

- It's never too late to make a *Little Brave Act*. You are not defined by the timeline society sets for you.

- Blooming later in life means you've had time to shed old skin, heal old wounds, and grow into the fullest, most authentic version of yourself.

- Late blooming as a pioneer means there is no template to follow, only your own. Your courage to bloom now will inspire many others. Quite often this is your second bloom.

- Late bloomers are proof that life's most profound transformations often come after periods of crisis, deep reflection and self-discovery.

- Late bloomers understand that true healing happens on its own timeline. Healing cannot be rushed.

Brave questions

- What fears are holding you back from fully embracing this new season of your life?

- What new dreams and passions are you discovering now that you hadn't noticed before?

- What gifts are you discovering within yourself now that you didn't recognise earlier in life?

- How can you honour the journey that has brought you to this moment of late blooming?

- How can you remain patient and trust the process of your unique, beautiful bloom?

Brave mantra

It's never too late.

PART 4
Pivoting

CHAPTER 10

The powerful little step of breaking the rules

'Recall how often in human history the saint and the rebel have been the same person.'

– ROLLO MAY, *THE COURAGE TO CREATE*

Are you ready to paint outside the lines and wander off the beaten path?

Living in alignment with your truth will at some point mean you have to dare to break some rules, defy the norms that seek to box you in – this is the only way to free yourself from the limitations of your initial Plan A and your backup Plan B. You don't have to go full rebel mode; that's not what I am asking you to do. However, there will be several defining moments in your life where taking unconventional and sometimes audacious actions will set your life on a new trajectory, one that you are meant to be on, one that will lead you to your own unexpected and soul-specific unique plan. This will involve the little step of breaking a few rules, shaking up some norms and turning your back on convention.

There are some rules we're supposed to break.

Firstly, there are the rules imposed upon us simply because of our gender. These are the rules that keep us small, that tell us we're less than, that confine us to narrow boxes of expectation. You know, the ones that try to cram us into tiny, suffocating boxes labelled 'proper ladylike behaviour' or 'macho manliness'. Who even decided that pink is for girls and blue is for boys? But we know better, don't we? We know that these rules are unjust, unequal and downright oppressive. And so, we rise up, we speak out, and we shatter them to pieces.

We must also acknowledge the intricate web of rules based on ethnicity, background and culture that seek to define and limit us, and we must be just as relentless in breaking free from those as well.

Then there are the rules that apply to everyone, regardless of gender, race, sexuality or socioeconomics. These are the rules so ingrained in society that we don't even question them. Things like the pressure to always be productive, the expectation to climb a career ladder or the idea that success is measured solely by material wealth. It's like we're all stuck in this giant hamster wheel, chasing after things that might not even make us happy in the end.

These rules are the invisible chains that bind us, the walls we've grown so accustomed to that we don't even see them anymore.

To free yourself from such rules, to find your innovative plan, you have to do some work. You have to challenge the status quo and listen to the voices of your gut and heart. These voices are the ones encouraging you to break rules, to start that passion project that may not make financial sense initially, or to leave your three children with in-laws so you can go on a meditation retreat. Listen to these voices. When you do, magic happens!

There are many ways to break the rules.

Challenging tradition

'Tradition: one of those words conservative people use as a shortcut to thinking.'

–WARREN ELLIS

When a tradition becomes an obligation, or stops our flexibility, we need to challenge ourselves to rethink whether it still has relevance to us. For example, when it comes to tying the knot, there's a whole lot of tradition and expectation thrown our way. But there is some wiggle room to create a ceremony that is unique to the couple, such as forgoing bridesmaids to let our pets take centre stage, or ditching the white dress for something more vibrant; but what about the rest? Is the tradition servicing us, or are we servicing the tradition? What if we look beyond the tradition, and ask ourselves what we authentically want? We can be surprised by the path that puts us on, and in the most delightful way.

Take my husband and me, for example – we challenged gender roles during our wedding ceremony with our mothers giving us away, instead of our fathers. At our reception, we also ditched a slow dance for a fully choreographed seven-minute mashup, complete with Michael Jackson's 'Thriller'.

While many of us make strides in challenging aspects of the marriage ceremony, weddings still remain the ultimate tradition-filled event with plenty of norms that go unquestioned. Why?

My friend Ange and her husband are in the wedding business. They've married over 2000 couples and have seen it all. And they've got this knack for knowing which marriages will stand the test of time and which ones won't. It's all in the little things: whether a couple looks lovingly into each other's eyes, or how patient they are when plans go awry, or the amount of physical affection they show each other. Ange and her husband have witnessed every traditional twist and turn, and I can attest that they have endless stories.

One Tuesday morning, Ange called, a hurried tone to her voice. 'Sheila, we need a witness.'

'What do you mean?' I asked, completely missing the context of her request.

'We have a couple getting married in a couple of hours and their witness can't make it — can you stand in?'

Two hours later, I was standing underneath the majestic Harbour Bridge as witness. I couldn't help but get a little misty-eyed, even though I had known the couple for five minutes; weddings, they're emotional.

As the couple were getting their photos taken, Ange then shared that she and her husband had their own little twist on the whole 'till death do us part' in their marriage contract. Instead of signing up for 'forever', every five years they renewed their wedding contract, and not with a white dress, but with an honest conversation. Crazy, right? They are traditional wedding-makers, but original disruptors to the traditional wedding!

Ange and her husband were being true to their desires as a couple, but I have to admit I was stunned. I had thought that a wedding celebrant would be committed to the tradition and philosophical norm that getting married was forever. The notion of 'forever' is not usually up for negotiation when you get married!

Ange explained that on the first wedding contract renewal they asked each other two questions: what do I love most about you? And what's not working?

Although most of us should of course be having this type of conversation regularly with our partners, setting this in a ritual context was an opportunity for real honesty, to work on the marriage and to constantly commit to the evolution of the relationship. It certainly kept both parties on their toes! It also provided them with an opportunity to leave the relationship and end the contract, if that's what they wanted.

Ange shared, 'In the lead up to each renewal period, we give ourselves the opportunity to decide whether anything was a deal breaker or not, such as not hanging up the bathroom towel. It allows us to get over things that are not important to argue over.'

As I reflected on Ange's story, I realised that saying, 'I don't want to commit to this forever' was a *Little Brave Act*. So much of a traditional life is about committing to something for eternity: careers, the cities we settle down in, our best friend relationships. But sometimes we have to quit, pivot and grow in a new direction. And you know what that means? Breaking norms, traditions and rules. Yes, it's going to make people uncomfortable, ourselves included. But here's the truth: half of us won't be doing the funky chicken dance on our 80th birthday with our beloved. Not all marriages endure. And not all traditions *should* endure.

Our Little Brave Act *may make sense to no one but ourselves.*

As for Ange and her husband, their little step was breaking the mould. By forgoing the 'forever' vow, they took themselves down an unconventional path and their marriage was stronger for it.

They have now had three contract renewals, and each time they grew more and more committed to having the best marriage they could.

Breaking norms to heal

'Finding the right healing path requires all or nothing. Once you place conditions on healing, all you can achieve is conditional healing.'

– CAROLINE MYSS

We need people to break the rules and shift the dial. Once the dial is shifted, we also need early adopters to grow and support movements, to create new norms and to find new ways for us all to heal.

Healing isn't about following some instruction manual or process. It's about getting down and dirty with the messy truth of who we are. Healing isn't pretty and more often than not, it's about confronting our demons head-on, even if it means defying convention along the way. There is beautiful chaos in healing because it's about finding our own path to feeling whole, no matter how unconventional that may be.

For 12 long years, I danced in intellectual rings with therapists, armed with all the fancy counselling frameworks I could find. I thought I had it all figured out. But then my therapy hit a wall. I experienced 'cognitive bypassing' – using my intellect to dodge my emotions.

Deep down, I knew I couldn't keep hiding behind theories forever. It was time to roll up my sleeves and confront the uncomfortable feelings I'd been avoiding. Yeah, it scared the hell out of me, but I also knew it was the next crucial step in my journey towards healing. Time to stop thinking and start feeling.

Your healing journey will be unconventional too, because it's the road less travelled that leads to the deepest transformation. You will need to blend the wisdom of the East with breakthrough therapies of the West. I have been there, done that myself. I have found myself ecstatic dancing in a yurt at the Esalen spiritual retreat centre in California, to help move energy through my body. I have also chanted the name of Krishna in a 10-day satsang retreat in India, to see the chaos of my mind. I have cried and wailed during a breathwork session as I released trauma in my womb. I have sent loving kindness to many in Buddhist retreats, to understand that unconditional love is within our reach. These were not mere experiences; they were pivotal steps unravelling another layer of the tightly wound mess that was me.

Can we let go of our ideals of what our healing journey will look like?

And there was ayahuasca. They say that one cup of ayahuasca is like a decade of therapy crammed into a single night. Can you imagine that? Aya-what-sca, you ask? Ayahuasca is a word that is hard to spell and even more difficult to pronounce. Ayahuasca is commonly known in the Amazon as 'la purge', and it's not for the faint of heart, that's for sure. It is a South American psychoactive brew made from an Amazonian vine and leaf with powerful hallucinogenic properties that claim to open your mind and heal past traumas. It is a medicine for the soul unlike any other.

When we share our forays into unconventional modalities, it can be confronting, triggering and foreign to those closest to us. And don't be surprised if they look at you like you've lost your mind! Especially if they are not on a healing journey at that point themselves. But that's just the price you pay for breaking free from the conventional path.

It was the price I paid when I wanted to try ayahuasca.

'You want to go where – to the Amazon?' my family and friends asked, intrigued. 'What is there in the Amazon for you? It is a dangerous place.'

This was back when I was still a finance director, and my family had a certain perception about who I was, which I of course enabled at the time. I simply didn't know where to begin with justifying where I was going or what I was doing, so I didn't. I knew I was breaking rules in order to heal. In their eyes it was unsafe, but my soul was yearning for this trip. At some level, the future was already present with me: I knew I would experience lasting benefits and tremendous healing. I couldn't find the words to make sense of it, but I knew I was ready to go.

Two months later, I was in the middle of the Amazon jungle perspiring heavily. My heart was racing as I took a big gulp of the foul-tasting and potent liquid elixir. The sludge trickled down the back of my throat; it would take 30 minutes for the effects to kick in. I had to sit back and wait. My heart started to thump.

Over a total of five ceremonies, I would projectile vomit, cry uncontrollably, shake furiously and purge my toxic thoughts. I released repeated patterns I had been holding onto, believing they served me and would keep me safe. I let go of unconscious patterns handed down through my ancestral lines. It was exhausting, illuminating and exhilarating all at once.

There is a spiritual protocol when engaging in an ayahuasca ceremony: a strict diet over a four-week period is required, avoiding salt, spices, red meat, alcohol and drugs in the lead-up to the ceremony. It is also recommended that you set an intention. Mine was: 'Show me my fears and how they do not serve me. Show me what true love feels like. Show me who I have become that doesn't serve me. Show me my life purpose.'

Ayahuasca put a spotlight on the parts of my life that were holding me back. I was shown the unconditional love offered to me by my family, which I had been too stubborn and blind to see. I realised I had been living my life with closed fists and not an open heart. I was shown how my negative, victim mindset had adversely impacted my life, and that I was fearful of living my life as my authentic self.

In this psychedelic haze, I could not turn away from reality: I had to sit for five hours each night in the great discomfort of my limiting and judgmental thoughts. The spiritual epiphanies were life-changing and the visions were extraordinary. There were visions of the potential of a life lived with no fear. I saw that to bring real love into my life required giving up my staunch independence. I loved my career and feared it would be compromised if I had a relationship in my life, which was not the case. I had to embody all the qualities I was looking for in the partner I wished to attract. During the ceremony, I was admonished for daring to believe I was unlovable, especially by my close family and friends. It was not that the love did not exist, but that I could not see it or receive it. This was a selfish part of my personality, the rejection of the love of family and friends.

At the end of the ceremony, I was flooded with feelings of unconditional love from my father. Up until this moment, I had foolishly felt that his love was conditional upon me being a 'good' and successful girl. With this limiting belief, I only attracted conditional and demanding love in my romantic relationships. I broke myself in order to be loved, then the relationship inevitably broke.

Finally, I was shown that my life purpose would involve a lot of changes, which would be uncomfortable, and I would need to surrender and trust the unfolding of new paths.

This healing journey in the Amazon accelerated the many needed changes in my life. Upon my return, I didn't share what I had experienced deep in the jungles. When I came back, many noticed a changed version of me. I was making better decisions; transformation was rapidly rolling through my life and my language was positive and calm.

One month after returning home, I made what I believed to be an unreasonable request of my boss: I asked to work four days a week. This was an overdue *Little Brave Act*. I wanted to go part-time so I could pursue my spiritual career. For months I had put off what felt like an impossible conversation. I was waiting for a 'no', expecting conflict and a combative argument. The many ways I had talked myself out of asking included justifying that no other finance director had worked part-time before. I didn't think my staff would support me and thought my boss would be irritated and annoyed.

However, as I embraced the first step of my unexpected plan, an unexpected answer came – my boss said 'yes'.

I had known that I had to go on a pilgrimage to a distant land and break the conventional norms of healing. Perhaps when breaking the rules we don't need to explain ourselves as much as we think we do. Perhaps we just need to heal in the wild, untamed way that only our hearts know how. The upgraded version of ourselves will be the proof that bucking the norms of healing can serve us.

Taking the road less travelled

'The older you get, the more you realize that it isn't about the material things, or pride or ego. It's about our hearts and who they beat for.'

– R.A. SALVATORE

Fast forward six years, and I found myself once again challenging the norms, this time breaking the rules not only that others had set, but that I too, had taken on. This time, it was about embarking on the deeply personal and transformative journey of starting IVF.

I made the classic mistake of googling 'Success rate of IVF for women in their 40s'. The dismal statistics didn't faze me, but the condescending explanation that 'women are focusing on their careers' did. Really? Let me share my truth. I didn't bury myself in my career because I was an ambitious workaholic. No, I used my career as a distraction from the deep, painful healing I needed to do. My drive for success was a symptom of unresolved trauma from my childhood.

When I finally faced my demons, I realised I didn't even know how to function in a healthy relationship. So, what did I do? I retreated back to the comfort of my career, where I knew how to navigate the world successfully. But here's the kicker: I chose to pursue IVF in my late 40s because I knew I wasn't ready to be the mother I wanted to be until then. That kind of self-awareness and dedication to personal growth should be celebrated, not criticised. It takes incredible courage to face your demons, to acknowledge you need time to heal and grow before stepping into motherhood.

But biology doesn't wait. And so, panic set in. There's this German word – 'Torschlusspanik' – that perfectly captures this feeling. It translates to 'gate-closing panic', that anxiety you feel as you watch time slipping away, taking opportunities and dreams with it. I felt that deeply.

The term has its roots in medieval times when towns had gates that were closed at night for security reasons. People who were late returning before the gates closed could experience a sense of panic at finding themselves potentially shut out and exposed to bandits and cold weather.

Over time, however, this fear of being 'shut out' became more broadly used to express the sense of apprehension or panic that can arise when one feels like time is running out for certain life goals or experiences, or the perception of diminishing opportunities.

Today, Germans use the term 'Torschlusspanik' to refer to a women's biological clock ticking. Isn't it amazing how the evolution of language can so closely mirror our collective limiting beliefs?

I remember feeling this way myself when the IVF doctors first told me that it was too late to have a child who was mine biologically. I nodded with silent internalised resentment and anger at my body and age for failing me. I felt gate-closing panic.

In the weeks and months that followed, however, I pivoted, I adapted and I got brave. I accepted that, while it *was* too late to have a biological child, it was *not* too late to have a child at all – if I pursued egg donation. A brave mindset is one where we are open to possibilities we never would have previously considered as a way to be resourceful. We break the normalised and sometimes rigid rules of life – because we have to.

I had already defied my culture's conventions by refusing to marry and have children early in life. I had already shaken up societal norms by sharing my fertility journey, on national television, peeing on a stick in front of millions. And I had already faced my failures, grieved them and learned to love myself anyway. But the dream of children lingered on my vision board. I still longed to get pregnant.

Egg donation was something I had never before contemplated. It broke the rules. It was unconventional. Being 'too old' did not mean that my motherhood journey was over. Of course, it didn't – because late never means impossible. Yet for so many people we associate late with the concept that 'the gate is closing'. We have been conditioned with an untruth: that if we haven't done something by a certain age, then it can't be done.

But what if we can find the strength and resilience to keep the gates open or find another way to reach our goals? What if we choose to break the rules and norms of society, even if they are taboo.

I chose to break those rules. I chose to believe that my path to motherhood was valid and beautiful, even if it didn't look like everyone else's. I embraced the idea that my child didn't need to come from my own eggs to be my miracle. I decided that 'late' was just another word for 'right on time' in my story. So, I opened my heart to the possibilities that egg donation offered, understanding that love and family are not confined by biology.

The gate isn't closing – it's opening to new ways of thinking, new definitions of success, new paths to happiness. And as I stepped through that gate, I found that the dreams on my vision board were not only still possible but were unfolding in ways more extraordinary than I had ever imagined.

Thinking outside the box

'Don't think outside the box. Think like there is no box.'

– ZIAD K. ABDELNOUR

Breaking the rules looks different for each one of us. Take my friend James, for example, a partner in a big law firm, living the corporate dream. When his lease came up for renewal, he had a lightbulb moment, asked himself some honest questions, and realised he was craving the freedom of van life, exploring the beaches of Sydney and working remotely along the way – and he wasn't even a surfer!

Then there was Kathryn, outgoing, sassy and financial stable, who decided to take matters into her own hands and become a single mother in her early 40s, despite not having a partner. It wasn't the traditional route to motherhood, it wasn't her original Plan A, and it wasn't her backup Plan B of waiting around for Mr Right to come along; but it was the right choice for her, and now she's the proud mama of a beautiful baby boy!

And then there was me, considering egg donation by a complete stranger.

At the end of the day, it's not about fitting into a box; breaking the rules is about embracing all the different parts of ourselves, even the ones that don't seem to fit together at first glance.

In breaking the rules, we get to question the status quo and ask ourselves, 'Is this right for me?' We also get to ignore the questions that don't serve us, the ones that keep us stuck in fear and uncertainty, such as:

What will other people think?

Am I doing the wrong thing?

What if it doesn't work out?

These questions are externally focused.

Instead, there are the questions that set us free, the ones that pave the way for *Little Brave Acts*. Questions like:

What feels like an aligned decision in this situation?

If I don't follow this decision, how does that make me feel?

What are my next steps that I need to take now?

The unexpected path will ask unexpected questions of you. Just asking such questions, and bravely answering them, is in itself a *Little Brave Act*, one that allows us to step onto an unexpected path.

When we ask ourselves brave questions, we are ready to listen to the brave answers.

Brave truths

- When you dare to break the rules, you open up possibilities for a life that truly reflects who you are.

- Your *Little Brave Act* may make sense to no one but yourself.

- True healing often means stepping away from conventional methods and trusting your intuition to guide you.

- When you feel uneasy about challenging norms, it means you are stepping out of your comfort zone and honouring your true self.

- You may feel the panic of running out of time - this is your opportunity to think outside of the box to find innovative solutions.

Brave questions

- Where in your life are you playing small to fit in, and what would it look like to step into your full power?

- What beliefs have you inherited from your family or culture that no longer serve you, and how can you begin to challenge them?

- How would your life change if you allowed yourself to dream beyond the boundaries of what's considered 'normal' or 'acceptable'?

- In what ways are you conforming to expectations that don't align with your true self, and what steps can you take to realign with your authenticity?

- Who in your life embodies the kind of bold, unapologetic living you aspire to, and what can you learn from their journey?

Brave mantra

I bravely defy the norms that don't serve me.

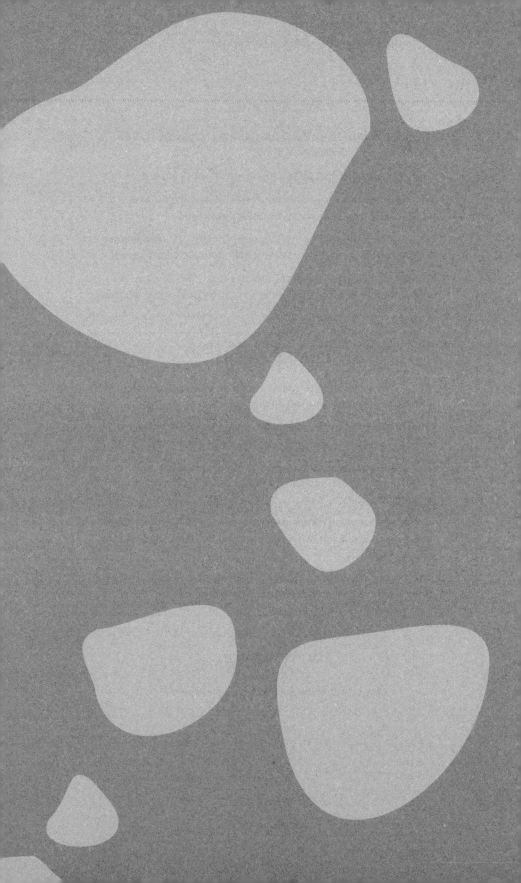

CHAPTER 11

Taking the unexpected path

'Biology is the least of what makes someone a mother.'

– OPRAH WINFREY

When Tyson and I finally decided to pursue egg donation, I must admit I was hesitant at first – and uncomfortable.

Here I was caught in the modern-day dilemma of swiping through profiles, trying to choose a shortlist amongst so many pretty young faces. I felt awkward, as my husband was cozied up next to me, playing the role of silent observer. I secretly wished he'd chime in with his two cents, but instead I was left alone with my thoughts – and let me tell you, they were not exactly sunshine and rainbows.

As I pondered which face to pick, I felt a pang of jealousy rise within me. Did my husband think these women were prettier than me? Was he attracted to any of them? These were uncomfortable thoughts to have, as we were deeply in love, and I never thought I would be in this position. It was as if someone had said,

'Surprise! Here's a plot twist you never saw coming!' This was our unexpected path, our Plan C.

The journey to choosing an egg donor and become a donor mother does not happen overnight. I had to settle into the idea. I had to accept that life never sticks to a script. I had to resist procrastinating over possible detours, all equally not pencilled into my Plan A or B. I had to stay focused on my vision board – where the original image of our happy family remained a constant. My head and heart were at war. But maybe, just maybe, I told myself, there would be a hidden gem waiting for me on this unexpected route.

Still swiping past donor profiles, my husband broke the uncomfortable silence between us with a quip, 'It's like Tinder for eggs, isn't it!' he joked.

I mustered a nod and sighed, attempting to find the humour in the situation. There were a couple of potential young women who had caught my eye, yet I hesitated to click the heart icon that would make my selection. The process was making my marriage feel a little crowded, like I was choosing a 'sister wife' to join us. And I again felt as if my older 46-year-old body and womb had severely let me down.

Still hurting after the launch of *Big Miracles*, I also couldn't shake the look our doctor had given us when our last fertilised embryo was found to have chromosomal defects and she suggested we consider a donor egg.

My mind, practical and exhausted, had whispered, 'Yes, this is the logical next step. No more heartache.'

Yet every other fibre of my being had felt like it had been numbed into silence. This is the first stage of grief, of course – shock, denial, wrapping its cloak around me, shielding me from the raw truth.

Every day I began to inch along the path towards acceptance, reluctantly embracing my new Plan C. But make no mistake, as I swiped through potential donor mothers, I was still navigating the early stages of this journey, feeling the weight of what might have been, while tentatively stepping towards what could be.

We all resist, revolt and resent our Plan Cs, until we realise that is the destination we were seeking all along.

Surrendering to Plan C

'I am learning to trust the journey even
when I do not understand it.'

– MILA BRON

After the failures of Plans A and B, the journey to Plan C is often a similar one, marked by fear, frustration and a sense of helplessness. We grapple with anger, sink into moments of depression, and wrestle with feelings of resentment. With each setback, there's a whisper in the back of our minds, asking us if our dream is slipping further out of reach. Are all of these setbacks a big neon sign from the universe, saying 'no'?

But here's the truth that life has taught me: when we cling stubbornly to the blueprint of Plan A or Plan B, refusing to budge even as the ground beneath us shifts, the universe finds a way of nudging us towards a different path.

When we face failure, especially when it feels like time is slipping through our fingers, it's natural to be consumed by a flood of self-doubt. We ask ourselves, 'Should I have tried harder, worked harder, pivoted faster?' We sift through the sands of our past decisions, questioning every turn, every choice.

In relationships that crumble, we second-guess ourselves, wondering if we should have fought harder, stayed longer. In business, we lose sleep ruminating over projects not going to plan, agonising over what could have been done differently.

It's a relentless cycle of hindsight, where the shadows of our past decisions loom large, casting doubt on our present and future.

However, when we muster the courage to pivot, adapt and recalibrate our plans, that's when we step onto the dance floor with the universe and start a graceful waltz with intuition.

I didn't realise it at the time, but even before our doctor had suggested egg donation to Tyson and I, my intuition had begun nudging me towards my Plan C, whispering that perhaps my original plan wasn't destined to unfold as envisioned. Signs of this realisation manifested as I found myself randomly googling alternative paths: 'adoption for older women', 'how to foster a child' and 'how do you buy donor eggs?'

Despite the seven cycles spanning seven months, I was obviously still desperately clinging to the hope that I could share the journey of parenthood with my beloved husband in some shape or form. For me, the ultimate dream wasn't tied to a specific genetic blueprint or a predetermined set of traits. While I had once daydreamed about mini-me with big eyes and a quirky sense of humour, I had to slowly realise that these details were inconsequential in the grand scheme of things. The absence of a child would leave a profound void within me, so I had to let it gradually transform me into the mother I longed to be.

It would take a multitude of little steps of course; and, when I finally surrendered to the path of donor eggs, it felt as though the universe was gently nudging me, whispering, 'Well done, darling. Your soul has been whispering Plan C all along. It's time to listen.' My Plan A and B may have been part of the journey, but they were never the destination destined to carry me towards my deepest desires.

What if Plan C was where your dreams lay all along?

Changing your mindset

'Gratitude unlocks the fullness of life. It turns what we have into enough, and more. It turns denial into acceptance, chaos to order, confusion to clarity.'

– MELODY BEATTIE

Let's be honest, the donor process feels like you're out in the Wild West of conception. Few have ventured there, and even fewer want to. But that's the point. I had to admit I was struggling. I needed to change my mindset, change the language of my thinking.

There had been a time when I was stepping into my *Little Brave Acts* with all the enthusiasm of a sloth on a Monday morning. My language was a dead giveaway – I kept saying 'I've got to.' Behind 'I've got to' was this sneaky little meaning of 'I don't want to, but I will do it anyway.' Now, sure, this can be the foundation of brave thinking, but with this language we're still running from and responding to pain. So, while this looks like courage, really it is fear in fancy dress.

Saying, 'I've got to have this conversation with my boss' still communicates that if I don't, things will just get worse. But when we reframe it to 'I get to', the emotion of empowerment kicks in.

You can use the 'I get to' reframe at any point when you realise, 'I don't want to be here, right now'. When we are stuck at an airport due to delays, going to the gym on a winter's morning or taking our kids to Saturday sports, the reframe can be:

'I get to spend extra time at this airport.' (Hello, people-watching and binging on snacks!)

'I get to go to the gym this morning.' (Yay, endorphins and the chance to not feel guilty about that extra slice of cake!)

'I get to take my kids to Saturday sports.' (Free entertainment and a chance to cheer like a maniac!)

Just saying these words is a way to pivot into what I like to call 'instantaneous gratitude'.

I really leaned on this kind of thinking when going through the donor process. One day, I switched from 'I've got to choose a donor' to 'I *get* to choose a donor', and it was like someone flipped the gratitude switch in my heart. I realised that, without this incredible woman on the other side of the world, my dreams wouldn't be coming true. She was giving me the gift of life. That's a hell of a lot better than trudging through with an 'I've got to' mindset.

When we change our mindset the impossible becomes possible.

After I made that language pivot, I found myself poring over photos on the donor website, hoping my child would inherit a big, broad smile, curious eyes, and gorgeous curly hair. The gratitude in my heart helped me embrace the process wholeheartedly, and I realised this was a beautiful part of my journey.

Flipping the script helps you embody this brave mindset. You might be surprised at how much it changes your perspective. It could make you laugh a little, breathe easier and even bring a sparkle to your day.

Trusting the divine plan

'The two most important days in your life are the day you are born and the day you find out why.'

– MARK TWAIN

One aspect that hadn't initially crossed my mind was the profound link between my Plan C and my life purpose. Tyson's and my journey unfolded on a public stage as we became the only couple featured across all three seasons of the television show *Big Miracles* between

2023 and 2025. As each show aired, more and more women reached out to me, hungry for insights into my experience, seeking solace and grappling with questions about IVF, egg freezing and the donor egg process. Over a million people watched the series; hundreds and hundreds of women sent me direct messages, each one a testament to the shared struggle of fertility.

In the midst of this whirlwind, something beautiful emerged. Women and men stopped me on the street, sharing their own battles with fertility. Often I could sense that it was their first time voicing their pain, frustrations and fear. In those moments, I became more than a stranger passing by – I became a confidante, a listening ear, a beacon of understanding – and a healing space would open between us. At other times, they were the ones offering support, love and connection and sharing their own miracle baby stories.

My husband and I even made appearances on the popular Australian morning show, *Today*, where we came to recognise the immense importance of encouraging vulnerable and honest conversations about fertility struggles. By speaking openly on such public platforms, we were contributing to a cultural shift, breaking down barriers and destigmatising a once-taboo topic.

When taboo subjects are brought into the light of prime-time television, they slowly lose their power to silence and shame. And in that transformation lies the seeds of healing and understanding, sparking conversations that ripple far beyond our own experiences.

I've come to realise that the twists and turns, the heartaches and disappointments of our tumultuous journey, were all threads woven into a grander design, one that required us to endure the trials, trust in the unseen path ahead, and simply step into each *Little Brave Act* at a time.

My husband is now a motivational keynote speaker too! His mission? To guide men towards becoming 'the next version of themselves' – conscious partners who can navigate the emotional terrain of fertility struggles with vulnerability and support. Having developed these essential skills and insights during our own struggles, he thoroughly enjoys sharing his journey with others.

Plan C is your purpose. Plan A and B was preparation.

For over a decade now, my vision has been to inspire women through bravery, to uplift them and guide them towards their own paths of empowerment. Little did I know the emotional toll this journey would take. As I reflect on the winding road that has led me here, I can see how every heartache and triumph was carefully stitched together, weaving towards my purpose. My journey through the failures of my Plan A and B were not detours; it was a vital chapter in the unfolding narrative of my life's purpose.

Ever heard the saying, 'Life is what happens when you're busy making other plans'? Well, ain't that the truth!

When Plans A and B unravel before our eyes, it's not a sign of failure, but an invitation, a beckoning to heed the call of our *deepest* desires, to traverse the path less travelled – the path of the soul. In that surrender, we discover a freedom that can only be found in embracing the unique journey that is ours alone to walk.

Once we accept that Plan C was always the plan, we can start anything new at any time. The smartest thing we can do is stay open, adaptable and be brave enough to know that the end result may look very different to our original vision, and there's a good chance it will be better. So, when your own Plans A and B derail, try to remember its only destiny rerouting you towards something far greater than you ever imagined. Trust in the divine plan.

Let me take you back to Erica, who came to see me feeling lost and bereft after her second husband Rob died. In the years that followed, Erica threw herself into studying mediumship, learning to communicate with Rob directly. She explored every spiritual modality she could find. She didn't just survive; she thrived. 'I started painting again – something I hadn't done in years. I walked the beach and golf course every day. I meditated daily, connecting with the universe, connecting with Rob.'

In one session, Erica shared, 'If Rob had lived, we would've had a good life. But I wouldn't have found this life of purpose. I know in my heart of hearts I'm on my true soul's journey now, unravelling gifts that have been locked away my entire life. I'm riding this rollercoaster of life and loving every wild minute of it!'

Erica now shares a home with her best friend. 'We've created our own little community. I've learned to lean on people. I have an active social life, more friends than I can count, and life is truly amazing.'

I asked her, 'What do you want to do with all the experiences and knowledge you've gathered over the last five years?'

She looked at me, eyes sparkling with determination. 'I want to be a death doula. I want to help women grieve and guide people to the other side.' Instead of dancing on her balcony, Erica has learned to dance to a different tune with a different rhythm. She continued, 'And you know what? I'm starting to think it may be time to love again.' Her gaze drifted into a distant memory, perhaps with Rob. 'Who knows? But I'm starting to feel ready.'

Lynne's powerful little step: sacred ceremony

'You are remembered for the rules you break.'

– DOUGLAS MACARTHUR

With deep trust, a strong vision and a clear mindset, we can allow the unexpected path to unfold in a way we couldn't have envisaged. This was the case for Lynne, an 80-year-old woman who had joined an online class I was teaching in mediumship and channelling. She had the curiosity of someone hungry for knowledge and, despite her age, she knew that she still had a lot of living to do.

Lynne shared with her peers, 'In my generation, the path was pretty much paved out for us: get married, have kids. It wasn't even up for debate.' Lynne's own journey took a different turn, however, because she didn't meet her husband until she was 43.

As the younger students listened, I could feel them pondering the challenges of blossoming into an empowered woman in the suppressive era of the 1950s and 1960s. The questions flooded in: had she wanted children? Had it been too late for her at 43?

She told us having children of her own had been her initial Plan A. Then she imagined the dynamics of having a 30-year-old child when she was 73. 'That wasn't ideal in my mind. There was a lot of rumination and vacillation before I decided, no, this wasn't right for me.' She accepted her Plan A had failed.

After the class ended, Lynne shared more of her story with me.

Lynne and her husband had found themselves in Oregon, making a fresh start, with a new identity. Previously resigned to the idea of not being a mother, their move sparked a renewed sense of possibility. With newfound time and energy, Lynne and her husband turned their attention to fostering. This was their Plan B, a compromise.

Still uncertain as to how motherhood would fit into her predictable and neat life, they envisioned a bright-eyed five-year-old walking through their door, bringing new life and joy into their home. Lynne dove headfirst into preparation, taking every class available to become a foster mom. She learned about the types of challenges foster children generally faced, including the scars they often carried from their troubled pasts. Despite the obstacles, Lynne remained steadfast in her commitment to provide love, support and stability to a child in need.

Six months after making the decision to foster, a 15-year-old girl arrived on Lynne's doorstep. She came from a history of abuse and neglect, having bounced around the foster care system for far too long. Teenagers, as any parent knows, can be a tough crowd to handle even under the best circumstances. With the formative years of bonding already behind them, Lynne found herself facing one of the most challenging situations a new mother could encounter.

Discipline issues arose quickly and forming a connection with her foster daughter proved to be an uphill battle. Lynne wrestled with the complexities of nurturing trust and understanding in the face of past trauma and resistance. Yet, despite the difficulties, Lynne remained committed to providing a safe and loving home for this vulnerable teenager, determined to make a positive difference in all their lives.

Lynne continued, 'When Heather turned 16, she wanted a car, and we wanted to help give her independence, so we bought one for her.' On the day of her birthday, she drove her new car to the foster home where she had previously lived. She had no intention of returning. 'That was extremely painful for me.' Lynne's voice trailed off into a heavy silence as she relived the memory.

Weeks later, a meeting with Heather's social worker offered little solace. Heather had made her decision; she wasn't coming back. And just like that, Lynne's time with her foster daughter came to an abrupt and agonising end.

Fast forward 15 years, and Lynne found herself scrolling through Facebook when a familiar face caught her eye. It was Heather – or at least, someone who looked remarkably like her. Lynne hesitated, unsure if it was truly her amid a sea of friends with Saudi Arabian names.

Summoning her courage, Lynne embarked on her own *Little Brave Act*, and in so doing set out on an unexpected path: she reached out to Heather. Curiosity mingled with apprehension as Lynne wondered how Heather's life had unfolded since their painful parting. Would she be met with rejection once again?

To Lynne's relief, Heather responded warmly. She was now married with three children of her own and living in Riyadh. What began as cautious messages soon blossomed into a deep and loving connection as Lynne and Heather navigated the complexities of their shared past.

After six months of heartfelt exchanges, they made the decision to meet in person once more, Heather returning to Lynne's family home where their paths had first crossed.

This initial visit was nerve-wracking. Lynne shared, 'This person had been part of my dreams and hope, and the reality was so different. So disappointing.'

As the visits between Heather and Lynne became more frequent, a momentum began to build in their friendship. With each passing year, they found themselves drawn closer together, forging a bond that both women wished had been possible 20 years earlier. It was a relationship that needed time to mature, to fully appreciate the depth of connection it could offer. But now, finally, the connection they had yearned for was within reach.

Lynne inhaled and paused reflectively, 'I felt it was wrong to call her my daughter, because she hadn't given me permission; but she *felt* like my daughter. So one day I plucked up the courage to have the conversation with her, maybe one that I wished had happened many years prior. 'I told Heather, "When you come to visit me, I tell people that my daughter is coming back, is that okay?"' Lynne recounted, her voice filled with emotion.

Heather's immediate response took Lynne by surprise. 'Well, I tell people I am visiting my mother!' In that moment, an unspoken truth was revealed, and Lynne and Heather found themselves echoing the same sentiment: 'You are my mum' and 'You are my daughter'.

Inspired by their newfound clarity and connection, Lynne, made another *Little Brave Act*, a bold request: what about making this legal, making it real?

This was Lynne's unexpected journey to motherhood, her Plan C. Her Plan A and B had failed, but by breaking the rules and thinking out of the box, she had achieved her dream.

Heather and Lynne embarked on the journey of legal adult adoption, navigating through the bureaucratic hurdles and paperwork. Along the way, they faced scepticism and raised eyebrows from friends and acquaintances. But amidst the legalities and administrative processes, they came to a profound realisation: the formalities didn't matter. What truly mattered was the love and bond they shared.

Over lunch one day, they discussed the idea of symbolically honouring their relationship. And so, they also began preparing for a ceremony – a celebration of their deep connection and enduring love – much like a wedding ceremony, but one between a mother and a daughter. It was a moment they had both longed for, a culmination of years of waiting and wishing.

I asked Lynne, 'How much has it meant to have someone say, "You are my mother"?'

'It's emotional. I can't find the words,' she whispered, her voice thick with feeling.

Her journey as a mother had been unlike anything she had ever imagined – a departure from tradition, a deviation from the expected. And yet, here she was, embracing a new kind of motherhood born out of bravery and defiance to challenge the norms.

As I reflected on Lynne's journey and the lessons it holds for us all, it gave me more confidence to embrace egg donation. Perhaps, my Plan C could work, because it was so unexpected.

Many Little Brave Acts *will lead you*
to your unexpected path.

Sometimes the most meaningful connections, whether with soulmate friends, soulmate mothers, or soulmate lovers, are forged on an unexpected path that we tread when our Plan A and Plan B fail us. It's a path that requires an unwavering belief in the possibility of our dreams, and one that asks us to challenge the traditions and norms we take for granted. As Lynne's story so beautifully illustrates, it's a path that can lead us to the most unexpected and profound blessings.

Speaking our truth

'Swim upstream. Go the other way.
Ignore conventional wisdom.'

– SAM WALTON, *SAM WALTON: MADE IN AMERICA*

An unexpected path also unfolded for Maggie Kuhn.

Back in 1970 in Boston, Maggie was forced to retire from her career at the Presbyterian Church at the age of 65, against her will. But she refused to let age or convention dictate the course her life would then take. She still burned with the fire of purpose, the vitality of youth pulsing through her veins, and a grand vision. When she was handed a sewing machine as a parting gift – can you imagine the nerve? – she didn't retreat into the shadows of retirement. No, she saw it as a call to action, a spark igniting the flames of her passion even brighter.

She decided to challenge the status quo. Infuriated by the injustice of being forced out of her job, she channelled this anger for good. In fact, she stepped into the spotlight of her life's greatest adventure. She gathered her friends, and together they birthed something revolutionary: the Gray Panthers, a powerful advocacy group dedicated to championing the rights and needs of older adults. The Gray Panthers would challenge ageism and fight for social justice, healthcare reform, and employment opportunities for seniors.

Maggie's fire, her charm and authenticity drew people in. As the momentum grew, the world started listening to what older folks had to say. She wasn't one to mince words or play it safe. No, Maggie stood firm, refusing to be silenced or sidelined. She demanded a seat at the table for the elderly, insisting that their voices be heard in decisions that mattered most.

Her work paved the way for significant advancements in policies and attitudes towards ageing, inspiring generations to come to embrace the richness and diversity of later life. And you know what? People listened. Congress listened. And, in 1986, they banned mandatory retirement for most jobs – a victory that changed lives and cemented Maggie's legacy as a true force of nature.

But Maggie's wisdom extends far beyond the halls of Congress. Her advice was to 'Leave safety behind. Put your body on the line. Stand before the people you fear and speak your mind – even if your voice shakes.' It's a rallying cry for anyone seeking to change their life, to make their voice heard, to stand up for what's right.

Can we take a leaf from Maggie's book and engage in the little step of speaking up, even when our voice shakes, when we can't find the perfect words, or when we stutter and stammer?

When we worry about the shake in our voice, we
lose connection to our message and purpose.

With each repetition of speaking our truth, we will become stronger, clearer and more confident. Breaking a rule at a personal level, can create a movement that challenges the norms, rewrites the rules and leads us towards an unexpected path – one where authenticity reigns and our lives can flourish in ways we never imagined.

Through my own years as a corporate trainer, mentor and keynote speaker, one truth has emerged with striking clarity: the most impactful voices, the ones that resonate deeply and spark real change, are often forged in the crucible of disruption. We spend more of our lives in the growth zone of life and less in the comforting embrace of familiarity. It's in these moments of upheaval, of discomfort and uncertainty, that we gather the pearls of wisdom and lessons that shape our understanding of the world; then we incubate those learnings and refine our insights that we may one day share them with the world. This path is not easy, but the rewards are immeasurable.

My Plan C

'What if infertility isn't a war but an awakening?
What if it's not about death but about a renaissance?'

– REKHA RAMCHARAN

When our Plans A and B crumble like gluten-free cookies, we're set free from the chains of expectation and societal 'shoulds'. Suddenly, our Plan C emerges – not as a mere backup plan, but as liberation. It's the path we were born to walk, unapologetically and authentically.

I found myself in the sacred space of a Zoom call with a well-known spiritual teacher and mentor, baring my soul about my journey using donor eggs. His story intertwined with mine in the most serendipitous way. His wife, too, had walked the path of needing a donor egg to build their family, and during that experience a wise shaman had told him that his wife was carrying a special child, and that 'this child wished to have two ancestral lines on the mothers' side of the family'.

In that moment, it was as if the heavens had spoken directly to my heart, as those were the exact words I needed to hear.

For years I had delved into the depths of my family's history, grappling with the weight of intergenerational trauma. Intergenerational trauma theorises that trauma can be inherited through a person's DNA. A part of me had always wondered how I might break the cycle and give my future children a simpler path forward.

Perhaps my journey with donor eggs could form a part of enabling that process?

As I broke free from the confines of tradition, I could not only feel a liberation from the rigidity of society's rules and must-dos, but also a release into freedom to perceive beyond the confines of my current life. Of course, the universe would ensure I found a donor with great meaning and connection for me personally, and of course it would ensure I furthered my desire to free the next generation of the trauma handed down. This insight created the space to consider how choosing a donor egg seemed so aligned for me.

Within renewed energy, I committed to the next step of the process.

She had a big, beautiful smile and eyes that said, 'I am ready to take on the world'. She described herself as a 'critical thinker'. Had I found my donor woman, who could help my husband and I bring our long-awaited child into the world? Her profile photo became my constant companion, a window into a world of unspoken hopes and untold dreams.

I hovered over her photo for a few weeks and spent several days looking at each of her profile photos, analysing her. After all,

I would potentially be carrying her egg inside me and continuing her genetic legacy – a mosaic of African American, Native American and French heritage.

Unanswerable questions ran through my mind, like:

What were her aspirations?

Did she have the warmth of a happy childhood, or did shadows lurk in the corners of her past?

What fears, if any, did she carry daily with her?

Would she ever think about me and us in the years that followed?

Would our paths ever cross?

Would my child look like her?

And then, with a trembling hand, and a heart brimming with anticipation, I pressed the appointment button to start the process to acquire her eggs, signalling the beginning of our magical, miraculous journey. I was ready. I added her photos to my vision board. This was my Plan C, and I was ready to embrace it with every fibre of my being.

Six weeks later, I had a donor egg implanted inside me. And the process of the infamous 'two week' wait started to see if I was pregnant.

On the day of my pregnancy test my two worlds collided – professional and personal.

There I was, basking in the glow of hosting the Women in Banking and Finance Awards, feeling like a boss lady extraordinaire. The awards are a pretty big deal in the banking and finance industry – I was staring out at over 600 faces, ready to address them as the ex-chief financial officer of an Australian publishing company, to tell them how I'd clawed my way to the C-suite in a sea of suits and ties, where women make up a mere 12 percent of the landscape.

As the women in the audience fixed their gaze upon me, I couldn't help but hope that they saw more than just a powerful woman.

I hoped they saw a reflection of their own resilience, their own tenacity, their own journey of triumph over adversity – a woman who had fought through limitations, glass ceilings, imposter syndromes, and made a throne for herself at the board table.

But amidst this polished façade of success – the glitz and glamour of the awards ceremony – I found myself teetering on the edge of anticipation, silently pleading with the universe for a miracle. I was smiling for the cameras, handing out awards with one hand; and with the other clutching the quieter, more intimate story unfolding within me – a story of hope, of longing, of the quiet desperation of waiting for the phone call that would change everything.

That's the reality of women who do IVF, you see – we're masters of the delicate dance between joy and heartache, between triumph and uncertainty. Life goes on, even as we grapple with the emotional turmoil of our fertility struggles. Our truth is one of resilience, courage and living a life unapologetically. Because whether I was crunching numbers in the boardroom or crossing my fingers in the fertility clinic, I was showing up with my whole heart, ready to take on whatever curveball life threw my way.

And the turmoil of my journey was once again set to be very public – the television crew of *Big Miracles* was filming my day. I had done a blood test at the IVF clinic earlier that morning and the call I awaited was from my doctor – to hear the results. She would call at exactly 3:30 pm, after the awards ceremony was over, just moments before she would jump in the taxi waiting out front to take her to the airport for her much-needed European vacation. Talk about timing, right? We're modern women on a mission, serving a greater cause – one that transcends borders and time zones!

Throughout the entire ceremony, the question of course hung in the air: was I pregnant? The signs were there – the snug dress, the swollen breasts. Given my age and that I was perimenopausal, I was on a very high dosage of hormones. But I had also had these symptoms with each failed cycle. I was no stranger to false alarms. So, I tempered my excitement with a healthy dose of scepticism, and waited for a victory that couldn't be measured in professional accolades, trophies, a shiny statuette or a plaque on the wall.

Eventually, the glittering lights dimmed, the vivacious chatter quieted, and the echoes of applause faded into the background as I retreated to the solitude of the conference centre's back room. There, in a sombre silence and heavy stillness, I shed the armour of my extroverted façade. My leg shook nervously as I finally had a chance to eat something. Then the doctor called.

Once more, the watchful eyes of the production crew turned towards me, their cameras poised to capture every raw emotion etched upon my face. Two years had passed since that fateful day when my first IVF pregnancy test had dashed Tyson's and my hopes. Two years of heartache, shattered dreams and clinging desperately to the fragile thread of hope that this time, just maybe, things would be different. And now, on the precipice of yet another pivotal moment, I found myself confronted with a question I dared not entertain: was I ready to hear the results?

Exhausted from the day of hosting, and so much hope resting in the next step, I was not ready. My heart was in my stomach. My eyes couldn't focus. Tyson reached for my hand and, in that moment, I wanted to be far away from that room . . . anywhere but taking this phone call.

But as the doctor talked, her tone shifted, and she sounded different from the other calls. My sixth sense kicked in. And I knew — whatever awaited on the other end of the line would irrevocably alter the course of our journey, for better or for worse.

'Sheila, you are pregnant!' Her words echoed in the stillness of the room, each syllable carrying a thousand emotions.

My ears rang with the deafening sound of shock. I sobbed all the tears that I had not yet released after trying to fall pregnant for so long. As my body collapsed into the safety of Tyson's arms, I realised that I no longer needed to be strong. At long last I had arrived at a new destination – one marked by the promise of new life. My Plan A, my Plan B *and* my Plan C had all led me to this moment of unimaginable joy.

You will only get to your Plan C after failing at Plan A and B.

A profound realisation washed over me then: that my donor child belonged to no one else but me and my husband. It was a truth that shook me to the core and taught me a lesson in love that was both unconventional and deeply profound. Learning to love in this modern, unconventional way was a journey of its own – one that stretched my heart in ways I never thought possible.

With each passing day that followed, I could feel my heart expanding with my belly, my soul growing alongside it.

Embracing this new reality meant navigating the complexities of parenthood with simplicity and grace. It meant rewriting the script of how we can become parents, and forging a bond that transcends biology and societal norms. In the midst of this beautiful chaos, I discovered a love that was uniquely mine – a love that knew no boundaries. And in that discovery, I found a sense of wholeness and fulfilment unlike anything I had ever known before.

This was the gift of my Plan C. The chance to become a mother.

Brave truths

- Plan C is your purpose. Plan A and B were preparation.

- You will only get to your Plan C after failing at Plan A and B.

- Many *Little Brave Acts* will lead you to your unexpected path. Sometimes, the best things in life come from the plans we never originally considered.

- Plan C is a reminder that there is more than one way to achieve your goals. It's a chance to explore new possibilities and discover strengths you didn't know you had.

- Committing to Plan C is about perseverance. It's refusing to give up on your dreams, even when the path looks different than you imagined.

Brave questions

- What are the most valuable lessons you have learned from your Plans A and B, and how can you carry those lessons into Plan C?

- How does it feel to acknowledge that Plan C is now your reality, and what emotions come up when you think about this new path?

- What strengths have you discovered in yourself through the process of adapting to new plans, and how can you use these strengths to succeed in Plan C?

- In what ways can Plan C open up new opportunities and possibilities that you hadn't considered before?

- What *Little Brave Acts* can you take today to begin moving forward with Plan C, and how can you celebrate each step along the way?

Brave mantra

I embrace my Plan C with bravery.

CHAPTER 12

The powerful little step of overcoming imposter syndrome

'I don't know whether every author feels it, but I think quite a lot do - that I am pretending to be something I am not, because, even nowadays, I do not quite feel as though I am an author.'

– AGATHA CHRISTIE

When we step into our bigger and bolder vision, many new opportunities start appearing in our lives. Our Plans A and B were cozy and more familiar, and now we are learning to get comfortable with our new and expanded life. While embracing our Plan C brings many unexpected joys, it also dredges up our self-doubt – that relentless voice whispering that at any moment, we'll be exposed as frauds. I'm sure you know the feeling.

You have poured your heart and soul into your work, given it everything you've got, and yet still feel like any moment now, someone's going to uncover the truth – that you're not as competent or capable as you appear. It feels like most of your accomplishments have been the result of luck – being in the right place at the right time. You work so damn hard to make sure that you never make a mistake. You are hypervigilant to make sure that no one ever discovers the real you. Because if they did, they'd realise you're not enough. It's a relentless cycle of worry, self-doubt and fear, draining your energy before the day has even begun. You're an imposter. I get it because I've felt that way too.

When we embark on the unexpected path towards our Plan C, we're highly likely to feel like imposters because we're breaking rules and navigating unchartered territory. So of course, we'll feel like we don't belong!

It's an uncomfortable feeling, and it can restrict us from fully embracing and stepping bravely into our Plan C.

But you're not the only one. The words 'woman' and 'imposter syndrome' go together like Bonnie and Clyde, Bert and Ernie, peanut butter and jam! In my coaching programs, when I ask women to raise their hands if they feel like imposters . . . almost every single hand shoots up. These are incredibly accomplished, successful women in leadership roles, yet they all feel unworthy, regardless of whether they're progressing with their life Plan A, B or C! Indeed, I work with many women in professional services – accountants, engineers, lawyers, IT consultants – and it's almost inevitable that they feel out of place in the male-dominated industries to which they belong.

As humans, we are programmed to belong and to feel safe. When we look around a room and can't see another woman, or a woman of colour, or a working mum, or an IVF mum, or someone from a group that we identify with, we don't see ourselves reflected in the dominant group. This can make us feel illegitimate, despite our accomplishments, qualifications or right to belong.

This feeling of not matching the dominant group can eat away at our confidence and sense of worth. For example, when we climb higher into leadership or inspiration roles, and look around to find fewer and fewer women beside us, it's like we're playing a game where the rules are made for someone else, and it chips away at our confidence, until we're constantly questioning if we really belong there.

I often felt the same in rooms full of pregnant women, not only as an IVF mum, but as a much older mum than those around me. I had such a different experience to everyone else, who was I to comment on how their pregnancies were going or the details of their birth plan? I felt like no one would even want to hear about my experiences – that my experiences lacked relevancy.

Unfortunately, the tighter the grip of imposter syndrome, the more likely we are to develop imposter *paralysis*. This is when we find ourselves shrinking, questioning our worth, asking for permission to speak, or not speaking up at all.

I've discovered that one powerful antidote to imposter syndrome is sharing our stories of feeling like imposters. So often we see a confident woman strut across a stage or our Instagram feeds, the image of perfection, style and accomplishment. But when she vulnerably shares her own struggles with feeling inadequate, there's a collective sigh of recognition from the audience. It's as if we're all thinking with relief, 'You too suffer from this painful affliction.'

When I see clients facing these challenges, I share a moment from my own career – when I was the new finance director at a publishing company. One of my early and main projects was relocating our warehouse. Two million books needed to be moved from one warehouse to another across two different states in Australia. I had never managed operations before, and the enormity of the task was daunting. So yeah, I was freaking out a bit and, just before a boardroom meeting to discuss my progress, I went to the women's restroom to calm my nerves.

Instead, my mind latched onto all the reasons why I was about to embarrass myself. In the boardroom, 12 men over the age of 50 were waiting. I didn't look like them, I didn't sound like them, and I was significantly younger than them. A cruel, berating, untrusting voice in my head kept whispering:

'They won't respect you.'

'Look at how much experience they have.'

'Why did you take this job when you knew you didn't have the experience for it?'

Every part of me wanted to leave the building screaming. Instead, I left the restroom and turned left towards the boardroom, my heart pounding, my legs feeling like they were made of lead.

As the meeting began, I could feel the uncertainty in my voice, and my thumping heart felt like it was beating in my throat. Then something miraculous happened – time suddenly slowed down. It was as if the universe had given me a reprieve to pull myself together. In that moment, I looked down at my thorough and well-planned notes and realised I *was* prepared. In fact, I was *over*-prepared. I may have felt like a fraud on the inside, but I had done the work, and I was an empathic listener who could easily facilitate the flow of robust conversation, healthy conflict and solution-based thinking.

Stopping and acknowledging our unique skills in the moment is a way to overcome imposter syndrome.

Over the course of that three-hour meeting, the energy in the room shifted. With each passing minute, I could see the unique skills that I brought to the table, and eventually I saw the unique skills everyone else brought too. We weren't just a bunch of boxes checked off for gender or organisational roles. Each person was a valuable contributor to the project, and it was clear that our combined strengths were going to make this thing work.

You know what? During that meeting, I *did* also fumble and stumble sometimes, and so did the other male attendees. Because here's the truth: you can't be 100 percent prepared for anything.

But you can 100 percent trust that every little step will take you further along the path you are meant to tread.

How to silence imposter syndrome

'Maybe we all have imposter syndrome and perpetually feel like our real life is right around the corner.'

– ANNA KENDRICK, *SCRAPPY LITTLE NOBODY*

Imposter syndrome doesn't just disappear when we hit a milestone. We tell ourselves that once we reach a certain point in our career, or shed that post-baby weight, or earn the right qualifications, or get closer to giving birth and becoming a mum at last, we'll finally feel confident and certain about ourselves. But that mindset is a set-up for failure. The source of imposter syndrome is an internal monologue that doesn't change unless we decide to change it.

It is a Little Brave Act *to change how we talk to ourselves.*

Sure, it might shrink over time as we near our goals; but then we level up, step into the growth zone again and give ourselves new goals. We seek out new job promotions, to lead a more accomplished team in sports, to speak on a panel with a bigger audience, or to talk to strangers about IVF – and just like that, the voice comes back, loud and clear.

The voice of imposter syndrome is something we need to learn to live with and manage. It's not about getting rid of it; it's about recognising it, understanding it and then doing our little steps anyway.

Whenever I was feeling like an imposter as an older IVF mum, like I didn't belong, I had to remind myself that I probably knew *more* about pregnancy than many others, given all the research I had done, and that my experiences were even more insightful because of it.

In an iconic interview in 2018, Michelle Obama herself dropped a truth bomb: she *still* feels imposter syndrome. Let that sink in: Michelle Obama still wakes up some days and battles imposter syndrome like the rest of us. Hearing this was a healing moment for many successful and ambitious women. She normalised it by saying, 'It never goes away.' When asked how she feels to be seen as a 'symbol of hope', she told the students listening, 'It *doesn't* go away, that feeling that you shouldn't take me that seriously. What do I know? I share that with you because we all have doubts in our abilities, about our power and what that power is.'

Thankfully, Michelle has not let imposter syndrome hold her back. It's an internal experience she has, but it does not affect her external actions. She still engages in *Little Brave Acts* daily and weekly, despite this internal struggle. Her example shows us that it is possible to feel doubts and still show up, still push forward, still make an impact. She teaches us that bravery isn't the absence of fear – it's acting in spite of it.

Even a few years ago, when I was at a Mind Body Spirit (MBS) festival surrounded by eager faces filling up the room, I was petrified of speaking about my expertise, of being seen as a fraud. Having attended numerous MBS festivals, I had absorbed wisdom from many spiritual teachers and witnessed the confidence with which they discussed mystical topics. Yet, here I was, preparing to speak as *an authority* on spirit guides and the art of receiving signs from the universe, and still my dear old imposter friend was making herself known to me.

I pressed on. For many years I had had a vision of speaking to spiritually awakened women and men, empowering them to embrace their spiritual gifts. My own journey had been challenging and isolating, so I was determined to support them in their awakening process. When this vision entered my heart and mind many years prior, I had not spoken on any big stages. There was no tangible evidence that this dream could ever become a reality. Yet it did, and it was. All I could do then was centre myself, remind myself of my expertise, and internally validate myself until I could accept that others would want to hear from me.

This process works for my clients too. They come to me after emerging from a crisis or a significant life change, feeling compelled to pursue a new venture: a creative passion, a side hustle, writing a book, launching a podcast or delving into a spiritual modality. Yet, early on in their journey, they are often abruptly stopped by the grip of imposter syndrome. I have observed this sudden onset of self-doubt inducing significant anxiety, especially as they've finally gained a clear sense of their purpose and mission; they're blindsided by this sudden surge of anxiety – sharing their story publicly, navigating the ever-intimidating world of social media or figuring out how to launch a website from scratch. This is precisely where learning to manage an inner imposter demon becomes crucial.

Journal writing is particularly useful when we need to clarify the new internal voice we want to cultivate. We can then confront the old voice with new language and reframe our perspective.

*The only way to stop feeling like an imposter
is to stop thinking like an imposter.*

One helpful question I ask myself when silencing that imposter voice is: 'What evidence is there that I have the knowledge and authority to speak?' Then, I would list all the places I had studied and the supportive teachers I had encountered. Next, I would shift the focus away from myself and reflect on how my talk would benefit participants. I could write several pages detailing the information I could share and how it could positively impact others.

Another helpful question is: 'What if I don't speak and cancel, how will I feel?' This can help to redirect your focus towards serving others *despite* your own emotional turmoil.

Lastly, I encourage my clients to contemplate how they would feel after delivering an inspiring and informative speech. When grappling with imposter syndrome, we often neglect to consider the potential for success and the opportunity to assist others, as we're preoccupied with self-preservation. But I could already feel the excitement build over the hour I delivered that spiritual talk. Midway through it, a woman raised her hand and enquired about ways to deepen her connection with her own spirit guides. As I offered her guidance, she bravely confessed her isolation in seeking a spiritual tribe, residing in a rural town with no like-minded individuals. Her vulnerability resonated deeply with me, evoking memories of my own awakening amidst the hustle of corporate life, feeling lost and uncertain about my path.

By the end of that session, a queue of spiritually awakened souls eagerly awaited their turn to pose questions. Their enquiries tapped into my expertise, honed over a decade of experience and countless transformative journeys. If I had allowed the grip of my imposter syndrome to cancel or diminish my voice, I would not have had the impact that my heart truly desired. This is the reward for overcoming imposter syndrome.

What if I had listened to my imposter syndrome voice as I wrote this book? You would not be reading it now, and I would not be able to share the progress of my personal Plans A, B and C with you!

The imposter within us disappears, when we
focus on who and how we want to serve.

Being bravely imperfect

'Perfectionism is not a quest for the best. It is
a pursuit of the worst in ourselves, the part that tells
us that nothing we do will ever be good enough.'

– JULIA CAMERON

As we proceed along our Plan C journey, we will of course seek to control it. After all the failed plans that came before it, we will want it to be perfect, because we haven't yet learned to trust that we are on the right path. So, don't be surprised when that inner perfectionist of ours pops up again, demanding a flawless execution. She's a tough one to silence.

We still need to learn to trust in our *Little Brave Acts*!

One of the topics I'm most often asked to speak about is being 'bravely imperfect'. It is such a popular topic because embracing our imperfections and giving up the charade that we are perfect can be one of the hardest things to do.

I demonstrate to the audience that this is something that we all face and that we are not alone with this internal battle. I kick off the conversation with a little game called 'Twenty questions', where I invite the audience to stand up and get ready to play along. The rules are simple: if the answer to any of my questions is 'yes', then it's time to take a seat.

Now, I'll admit that the first question I ask is a bit of a set-up: 'Please sit down if you've ever, ever in your life, made a mistake.'

Cue the nervous laughter, the hesitant murmurs, and the collective discomfort as each person in the room slowly settles back down into their chair.

Everyone starts out in this game with one goal in mind: to win. But as the first question is asked, it becomes painfully clear that there will be no winner. We're confronted head-on with our discomfort around the very idea of making mistakes, and it's a powerful eye-opening moment for everyone involved.

Perfectionism is the cousin of imposter syndrome. To avoid failure, an imposter sets an exceedingly high bar for themselves. They over-prepare, overwork and strive for perfection. Yet, paradoxically, this pursuit of perfection only reinforces feelings of inadequacy, because it is an impossible pursuit and fuels the belief that we are not deserving of our accomplishments.

Perfectionism does not make you feel
perfect. It makes you feel flawed.

During the years when my imposter syndrome was at its peak, I struggled to receive constructive criticism. When I did receive feedback that could potentially elevate my development, help me understand my blind spots and improve my relationships, I would take the feedback poorly – picking it apart and then myself. It would rattle me and I would spend weeks ruminating. As a result, I would avoid constructive feedback, or search for verbal validation. For an imposter, feedback is destructive instead of constructive.

These are powerful truths to remember when we're embracing innovation and breaking rules on our Plan C journeys. There will be uncertainties. We will make mistakes. But as long as we focus on stepping into one *Little Brave Act* at a time, we can trust that they will all culminate to take us where we need to go.

Reframing imposter syndrome

'Imposter syndrome is just another term for growing pains.'

– GLORIA STEINEM

Let's dive into this idea of reframing imposter syndrome, because it's time we saw it for what it really is – a sign that we're levelling up in life. When that familiar, uncomfortable feeling that we're not good enough flares up, it's not a signal to retreat; it's proof that we're on the cusp of a breakthrough, that we're being brave and stepping into new territories of growth.

I was recently swapping notes with fellow career coach, Alice. Alice is inspiring – she specifically coaches successful women, many of whom feel like imposters. She shared, 'I tell my clients, the moment you experience imposter syndrome, embrace it. It's a sign that you are on the verge of transformational growth.'

Alice and I were talking about how heartbreaking it is, as coaches, to see talented women self-sabotaging themselves, right when they're about to land the job, get the promotion or earn the pay rise they deserve. We chuckled as we shared our own deep-seated insecurities too. Both of us had quit our corporate jobs and, as we started our coaching businesses, were plagued with daily insecurities. In fact, that's how we met – bonding at a networking event over how hard it was to promote and sell ourselves. It's a shared struggle, but it's also what makes us so passionate about helping other women navigate through it.

She continued, 'I see good candidates getting passed over because they can't sell themselves on their CV or in an interview.

They're too scared to ask for a pay rise because they fear hearing "no", feel like they don't deserve it, or think they can't ask for that much.'

Valerie Young, author of *The Secret Thoughts of Successful Women*, flips the script on imposter syndrome, not viewing it as a negative, but as evidence that you're challenging yourself and making progress. As she puts it, 'Imposter syndrome is a natural consequence of success. If you're not feeling it, you're not growing. It's a sign that you're pushing your boundaries and stepping out of your comfort zone.' This mindset turns the nagging feeling of imposter syndrome into a clear signal of personal development.

Let's not forget where this all started. The term 'imposter syndrome' came from a study, 'The imposter phenomenon in high achieving women' by Pauline Clance and Suzanne Imes. They interviewed 150 highly successful women and every single one of them – yes, 100 percent – reported feelings of imposter syndrome. It's a universal struggle, but it's also a sign that you're on the path to something greater.

See, our job isn't to suppress, eliminate or even overcome imposter syndrome. It's a hallmark of being a successful and ambitious woman. The evidence is irrefutable.

The real problem isn't the imposter syndrome itself; it's the negative, critical and doubtful voice that tags along with it. The problem is that we listen to that voice and believe it. We need to press the mute button on that voice, so we can hear another voice that is also within us – the one that believes we are worthy and capable and can achieve our dreams.

I asked Alice how she dealt with imposter syndrome.

'There are two sides to me,' she replied. 'There's the imposter, and on the other side is the superwoman. They coexist. I make sure that I listen to the voice of the superwoman because she helps me run a successful coaching business.'

Even when I'm a mess
I still put on a vest
With an S on my chest

– ALICIA KEYS, 'SUPERWOMAN'

Our little step here is adopting a new internal voice. A voice that allows us to reframe negative feelings to see the positive – the voice of our inner superwoman. The one that says:

'Yes, I feel like an imposter and I am constantly learning and growing.'

'Yes, I feel like I am an imposter and growth happens outside of my comfort zone.'

'Yes, I feel like an imposter and pushing my limits brings me closer to my goals.'

When we change our inner monologue, we can walk forward *with* imposter syndrome instead of stopping in our tracks or procrastinating.

Achieving our goals and stepping into Plan C will likely come with the uncomfortable feeling of imposter syndrome somewhere along the way. So, the next time that imposter voice whispers in your ear, let your superwoman voice speak louder. Let it remind you of your strength, your resilience, and your unwavering commitment to your growth and success.

Brave truths

- Can we accept that imposter syndrome is universal: most of us have felt like frauds at some point, and you're not alone in this - even the most successful women doubt themselves sometimes.

- If you're feeling like an imposter, it means you're pushing your boundaries and stepping into new, challenging territories. Growth is uncomfortable but necessary.

- The only way to stop feeling like an imposter is to stop thinking like an imposter.

- Trying to be perfect only fuels imposter syndrome. Perfectionism does not make you feel perfect. It makes you feel flawed.

- Use positive affirmations to remind yourself of your strength and capabilities; rewire your thinking with words of love and encouragement.

Brave questions

- When have you felt like an imposter in the past, and how did you overcome those feelings?

- What unique strengths and talents do you bring to the table that no one else can offer?

- How would your life change if you fully embraced your worthiness and stopped questioning your place in the world?

- How can you reframe your thinking to see imposter syndrome as a sign that you are growing and pushing your boundaries?

- Who are the people in your life that support and believe in you, and how can you lean on them for encouragement?

Brave mantra

I am worthy of my dreams and capable of achieving them.

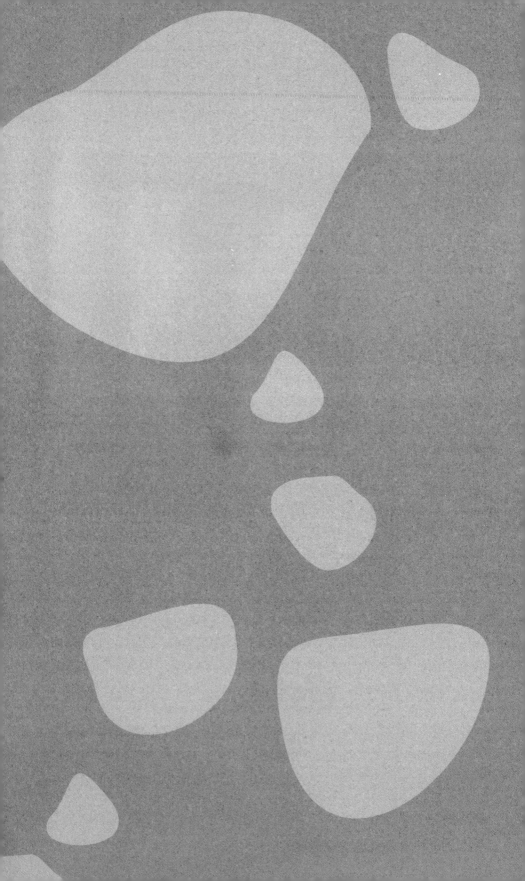

CHAPTER 13

Staying the course when things get tough

'Enthusiasm is common. Endurance is rare.'

– ANGELA DUCKWORTH, *GRIT: THE POWER OF PASSION AND PERSEVERANCE*

Stepping into Plan C is never the end; it's just the beginning of a new chapter. And let's be clear: you're going to need to summon every ounce of bravery you have. You've faced the fatigue of multiple failures or prior plans, and yet, here you are, ready to commit to a new path. That's the grit and resilience we're talking about.

True transformation doesn't happen overnight, it will require sustained effort over time. It won't be enough to have a single breakthrough or moment of clarity; true growth demands consistent effort and dedication. Commitment to doing the work means showing up every day, even when progress feels agonisingly slow or setbacks try to knock you off course. This is where the real work happens – where you pivot and develop that brave mindset that keeps you moving forward.

Each day presents a new opportunity to confront our shadows, integrate our past wounds and cultivate your highest self. This ongoing process of self-examination and self-improvement is vital. It keeps us aligned with our core values and purpose. Every little step we take, no matter how insignificant it may seem, is a vital part of our overall journey of recovery and transformation. This is how we stay the course. This is how we build the life we've always known we were meant to live.

Master your mind, master your life.

Understanding that tough things happen

'Sometimes when you are in a dark place you think you have been buried, but you've actually been planted.'

– ANON

Along the way we will hit turbulence. Whenever we enter a winter season in our life, our task is twofold. First, we must find the light so we're not completely dragged down by the darkness. This might mean finding small moments of happiness. Second, we also need to allow transformation to occur, which means vacillating back into the alchemy of darkness and letting it work its magic.

This is a delicate balance. It's about holding space for both the light and the dark, embracing tough times while still seeking out the little sparks of joy. Because it's in this balance that we find our true strength and resilience.

Let's look to Sweden for inspiration, as people there live with some of the darkest, longest winters, and yet are consistently ranked among the happiest people in the world. How do they do it, and what can we learn from them?

Kiruna is the most northern town in Sweden. On the shortest day of the year, the sun barely makes an appearance, rising at 11:00 am and setting at 12:30 pm. That's right, a whole hour and a half of daylight. In the depths of winter, the Swedes endure more than their fair share of darkness. But they've got a philosophy to combat any seasonal depression that creeps in – a little concept called '*Koselig*'.

Koselig is a positive wintertime mindset, and it is all about finding light in the darkness. It's about embracing the cold, hard months and making them a bit more bearable. Koselig is not just about bonfires and warm beverages – the philosophy is psychological as well as physical. The Swedes can teach us that, just because it's pitch-black outside, doesn't mean you can't create some light within.

So, when life feels dark and you're struggling to find your way, remember the Swedes and their Koselig. Light a candle, brew a batch of cacao, get out your tarot cards and invite over a friend – find joy in the little things. Because if the Swedes can find a way to thrive with only 90 minutes of sunlight, then so can you.

Finding the light

'Strength does not come from what you can do.
It comes from overcoming the things you
once thought you couldn't.'

– NIKKI ROGERS

The feeling of a 'winter darkness' comes in all shapes and sizes, and at different times of our lives. For me, it showed itself during my IVF journey.

IVF involves a relentless series of injections – whether to monitor hormone levels or adjust them. Anyone who's been through it will tell you, the first thing that comes to mind is the pain of too many needles.

I vividly recall my first blood test at the IVF clinic. I arrived early, excited that my journey to conception was officially beginning. I was the fourth person in line behind a row of women who, upon reflection, looked depressed, beaten down and introspective. I was the opposite – chirpy, hopeful and positive. That's how we all start our IVF journeys.

That morning, I was in a chatty mood. I turned to the lady next to me and introduced myself, asking her which cycle she was up to.

She flatly replied, 'This is my fourth.'

'Oh,' I replied, trying to find a way to lift her spirits. 'How is it going?' I asked, though I already sensed the answer.

'In my last cycle, we didn't even get one egg.'

The conversation ended there. I stared down at my sneakers, uncomfortable with making eye contact. The ladies returned to mindless scrolling on their phones, a distraction desperately needed to numb themselves.

Fast forward by five months, and there I was, standing in line, numbing myself with the same mindless scrolling. My cheerful optimism had given way to the all-consuming reality of IVF. I was now on my fourth cycle and starting to experience fertility burnout.

IVF presents a gauntlet of challenges: anxiously waiting for the nurses to call, only to receive disappointing news; cancelling exciting plans when they clashed with essential procedures; nervously sitting with our financial planner, wondering how many cycles we could afford before our savings were depleted. Amidst this emotional rollercoaster, my husband and I constantly reminded each other that we had chosen this path. At our age, this was our only chance to conceive a child. So, we had to endure and be prepared for whatever the process demanded.

This didn't take the pain away, and yes, I did still experience many moments of depression and anxiety. However, I was able to function, thrive and move beyond the 'wintery' emotions that I was experiencing. I tapped into my inner Koselig and found the light in the darkness. I danced wildly in my living room, allowing my body to express what words could not. I allowed myself to laugh deeply with my friends. I binge-watched old favourite Netflix series. I allowed books to transport me to other worlds, where my inner spirit could roam free. I surfed guilt free during hours where I could have been working. These were small and important *Little Brave Acts*.

When we embrace the mindset that tough things do and will happen, we become more resilient and quickly move away from a victim mentality.

Instead of asking, 'Why me?' I adopted a brave mindset and then started asking more empowering questions:

How can I take better care of myself right now?

Who can I lean on for support?

What can I learn from these challenges?

This pivot in perspective helps us recognise that challenges are an inherent part of our journey. When we choose the journey, we choose the rewards and the adversity at the same time. Embracing this duality makes us stronger and more prepared for whatever life throws our way.

Grit: when you hit the wall

'When you keep searching for ways to change your situation for the better, you stand a chance of finding them. When you stop searching, assuming they can't be found, you guarantee they won't.'

– ANGELA DUCKWORTH, *GRIT: THE POWER OF PASSION AND PERSEVERANCE*

Sure, we can endure hardship when we can see a clear path to success and when we know there is a reward waiting at the end of the journey. But what if that success isn't guaranteed? What if we're faced with uncertainty, with doubt, with the nagging fear that our efforts might all be in vain? What then?

I've been asked by many women, 'How did you endure so many rounds of IVF when there was no guarantee it would work?' My answer is simple: some goals demand tenacity. Some dreams require us to dig deep, to tap into our grittiest selves, and to keep pushing forward, no matter what the odds. Some visions ask us to continue to rechart a new course – and adapt. It's not a straight path; it's a winding, twisting journey that demands flexibility and resilience. You have to be willing to bend without breaking, to find new ways to move forward when the road is blocked.

During these moments, we need to bite down and endure. We need to summon our inner strength, to remind ourselves why we started, and to keep our eyes on the prize. When we've identified our purpose, our calling, our next right step, we need to harness the power of grit. Why? Because deep down, we know that this is the way forward, even when it's hard, even when it's uncomfortable, even when it feels like we're fighting an uphill battle.

Now, let me be clear: when I talk about grit, I'm not talking about blindly sticking to our plans. I'm talking about sticking to our vision, our greater purpose, even in the face of adversity. Grit is what keeps us open to new options, new alternatives, even as we hold fast to our ultimate goal. It is grit that carries us to our Plan C, our unexpected path.

When I was going through IVF with my own eggs, I refused to see it as my only option. I stayed rooted in my vision, believing that there was more than one path to motherhood. I explored surrogacy, donor eggs, fostering and adoption – all while staying open to new possibilities, new opportunities.

And let me tell you, it wasn't easy. It took late nights scouring websites, many Zoom calls with others ahead of me on the journey, months of listening to fertility podcasts. But through it all, I kept that fire burning inside me – the fire of belief, of determination, of unwavering faith that my efforts would shape a brighter future – one with a family. It's the difference between hoping for a better tomorrow and resolving to create it.

So, yes, grit saw me through 10 rounds of IVF in 18 months. But more than that, it reminded me that, when we tap into our inner strength, when we trust in our vision and keep pushing forward, there's no limit to what we can achieve.

Dreams never die, they just become unlived

'Never give up on a dream just because of the time it will take to accomplish it. The time will pass anyway.'

– EARL NIGHTINGALE

The setbacks we encounter when we're chasing our dreams can feel like punches to the gut, leaving us reeling and questioning everything we thought we knew. They can make us doubt ourselves, our abilities and whether our dreams are even worth pursuing. And let's be real – they hurt. They hurt like hell.

But here's the thing: setbacks are a part of the journey. They're not the end of the road; they're just a detour. The journey to fulfilling our dreams will never be easy or smooth. But it's not the setbacks that define us – it's how we respond to them.

There are dreams buried within all of us that are unlived, waiting to be unearthed and given life. It takes courage – those little steps – to excavate these dreams from the depths where we've hidden them. You know the ones I'm talking about – the ones we've tucked away because we think we don't have the time, money, energy or freedom to pursue them. As we grow older, those dreams can start to feel like frivolous fantasies, like something we should have outgrown by now. We tell ourselves that chasing our dreams is selfish, indulgent or simply not practical. So instead, we bury them underneath a pile of laundry and a couple of kids. And what do we do then?

Well, we might find ourselves resenting those who have the audacity to chase their dreams, or we might try to live vicariously through our children, hoping they'll fulfil the dreams we've abandoned. Or maybe, just maybe, we convince ourselves that those dreams were never really there to begin with – we stop talking about them altogether.

Staying stuck in our comfort zones might feel safe and cozy, but it's also soul-sucking. It's a slow death by mediocrity.

Dreams may seem lofty because they challenge us in ways nothing else can. They require us to step into unfamiliar territory, to develop skills where we have zero competency, to pioneer a path where no template in our family existed before. They often demand financial investment and emotional risk, with no guarantee of success. Dreams are the outliers on the bell curve of life, defying the norms and expectations that society sets for us.

Our dreams quite often defy logic, so a deeper understanding of their nature helps us understand why so few of us pursue them, or delay doing so.

The first reason lies in what psychologists call 'automatic negative thoughts' (ANT). These are random, negative thoughts about ourselves that plague the average human brain, which churns out up to 70,000 thoughts a day, the majority of them being negative. Imagine, then, what happens when we entertain the idea of living our dreams; those negative thoughts spiral out of control:

'What if I fail?'

'I can't disappoint people.'

'I don't even know where to start.'

'This feels too hard.'

'I'm too old for this.'

We relegate our dreams to the realm of wishful thinking, with the safe refrain, 'One day I will . . .'

The second reason why we hesitate to pursue our dreams is our fear of the unknown. Uncertainty can trigger the primal instincts of fright, fight or freeze. A study from University College of London discovered that uncertainty induces more stress than certain pain. Participants who knew they'd receive a painful electric shock felt calmer than those who were uncertain, even if they had a 50 percent chance of getting shocked, and thus a 50 percent chance of not getting shocked. Dr Robb Rutledge, the study's co-author, explained that it was uncertainty making participants anxious, seriously anxious – so much so that they would prefer the certainty of an electric shock!

Now, apply this to pursuing a dream – where every step shrouded in uncertainty amplifies our anxiety. We crave assurance of success, or at least an understanding of how to navigate potential failure and its aftermath. The anguish of uncertainty at each milestone of chasing a dream becomes too overwhelming to bear, explaining why many of us don't pursue them. There's perhaps no greater unknown than the journey towards realising a dream.

As an eight-year-old, I had a dream of learning how to surf. For years, my dream waited patiently for me to be brave. It wasn't until I turned 29 that I realised I couldn't learn how to surf on my own. So, I made my first little step of my *Little Brave Act* – I dialled up the local surf school and booked my first lesson. It was way outside my family's comfort zone. My parents didn't know how to swim, let alone navigate the at-times frightening surf conditions on most Australian beaches.

The day of my first surf lesson rolled around quickly – a clear Australian summer morning at Cronulla Beach. I was so excited when I was handed my blue 'foamie' surfboard and we headed into the surf. Learning to surf is a messy, humbling process – one that's full of wipeouts, frustration and swallowing mouthfuls of saltwater. Yet, amidst the struggle, there was magic – a fleeting moment where I caught a wave, a feeling of pure elation that made it all worthwhile.

I thought this was the start of me embracing and working on this dream. But it wasn't to be. On that perfect summer morning, while I was battling the waves, the infamous anti-migrant Cronulla riots ignited, fuelled by anger and prejudice. When I clambered from the water, I suddenly felt unsafe. I walked through the chaos of 5,000 people expressing their contempt for anyone who looked foreign. For a brown-skinned girl chasing a dream, I was in the wrong place at the wrong time. As we pushed through the crowd, a young blond guy shouted to his mate: 'Nah, leave 'em, they're just lucky they've got surfboards with them.' I didn't look back and I didn't return for another lesson.

Regardless of your dreams, when you set out to pursue them, you are chasing that initial rush – the thrill of having a new customer, or your first subscriber to your YouTube channel, or stepping onto the plane for your European vacation. In that moment, you feel the most alive; you *know* you are defying the gravitational pull of your old life and you are starting to do something extraordinary with your life. It's a moment of exhilaration – a confirmation you're on the right path, defying the limitations that once held you back.

The thing with chasing our dreams is that we start out in calm, perfect conditions. We embark on our journey with optimism, blissfully unaware of the storms that lie ahead. We don't anticipate bad weather that will test our resolve, or being caught in a dangerous rip that will threaten to drag us under, or the repeated setbacks that will knock us down many times. We're blindsided by the reality that our side-hustle business may struggle to turn a profit, or that launching a YouTube channel will demand long hours of solitary work, exposing our deepest insecurities, or that there might be multiple flight delays and lonely moments as we backpack around Europe. And it's in the face of these challenges that many of us choose to quit, overwhelmed by the daunting task of overcoming adversity.

Boldly taking little steps to chase our dreams isn't just about overcoming personal internal obstacles, it's about confronting external systemic obstacles that can thwart our progress and crush our aspirations. These limitations can feel insurmountable, leaving us feeling like the odds are stacked against us and the battle to keep our dreams alive is simply too daunting. We find ourselves uttering statements like:

'I can't become a CEO, because the corporate world will never change its attitudes towards women.'

'I'll always face racism, regardless of my qualifications.'

'My body will never be accepted.'

'It will always be challenging for me because of my upbringing.'

'I'm too old to be considered for employment opportunities.'

'My eggs are too old for me to be a mother.'

The danger lies in succumbing to a collective sense of victimhood, where we resign ourselves to the belief that external circumstances will forever dictate our fate.

I consider myself fortunate to have been raised by a brave man, my father, who looked beyond any societal limitations – gender and race included. He instilled in me the belief that excellence transcends such superficial barriers. His words often echoed in my mind as I pursued my corporate dreams: 'Sheila, if you are the best at what you do, you will always have a job. You will never have to worry.'

Inspired by him, another dream I had was to reach the C-suite in finance – a realm that few women had reached. My internal mantra was, 'I am going to have one of those positions.' Nine years of unwavering dedication later, I was appointed as CFO at a prominent publishing house.

Through the momentum of many little steps building towards *Little Brave Acts*, we all have the power to overcome the systemic obstacles of racism, ageism, sexism and socioeconomic barriers. We can't let our dreams die just because we encounter resistance – because we will inevitably experience resistance when chasing our dreams.

Succeed not despite of who you are, but because of who you are.

For this reason, 15 years after the Cronulla Riots, I picked up a surfboard again. My dream to surf had never gone away; it was just waiting for me to get brave again, and that's exactly what I did.

You see – dreams never die, they just become unlived.

But now I was waging a different kind of war, a war against my age. This time I wasn't 29, I was 44, with creaky joints, tight muscles and a lingering fear of the ocean! One important thing had changed, though, which is that I had learned the power of little steps. From seeking out a surf coach to braving pre-dawn sessions alone and confronting the biting chill of winter swells, each *Little Brave Act* I took towards my dream served as a testament to my resilience and determination.

In the end, it wasn't just about conquering the waves; it was about reclaiming a piece of myself that had been lost to fear and doubt.

Now, you might be expecting some grand finale in the tale, with me becoming an Australian champion surfer! But no, that was never the point. My goal was to just to learn how to surf, and I did. After a year filled with countless *Little Brave Acts*, I mustered the courage to embark on an all-girl surf retreat in Bali. And, let me tell you, it was an adventure of a lifetime. Despite being affectionately nicknamed 'Boomer' by my fellow surfers due to my age, my spirit was youthful and alive. I had the time of my life out there on those waves.

Kris's powerful little step: hard doesn't mean impossible

'Healing may not be so much about getting better, as about letting go of everything that isn't you — all of the expectations, all of the beliefs — and becoming who you are.'

– RACHEL NAOMI REMEN

Learning to surf at 44 isn't easy, but it's a walk in the park compared to being thrown off your bike, over the top of a car, onto the operating table and waking up not knowing whether you will ever function again. This was the beginning of Kris's transformation.

Kris wanted to work with me on mindset coaching, and from the start I was struck by her arsenal of tools. She was a gut health expert with an incredible story. At just 23, she had found herself in a nightmare beyond anything she could have imagined. One moment, she was speeding along with her boyfriend on his motorcycle, and the next they collided with an oncoming car. She was flung 10 metres over a car. She woke up alone in an ER in England, engulfed in the most excruciating pain of her life, with no family or friends by her side.

Kris was placed in a drug-induced coma for seven days, while her boyfriend – the one responsible for the accident by speeding in a bus lane – walked away with nothing more than a wrist sprain. Her parents flew to her side, only to be met with the devastating news: if she survived, she would likely suffer severe brain injuries. She had a tear in her brain, a skull fracture, four broken ribs, a punctured lung, a perforated eardrum and a broken collarbone.

Life, in all its brutal unpredictability, had thrown Kris into the deepest, darkest waters, and now it was up to her to find the strength to swim through them.

In the weeks and months that followed, Kris had to relearn everything, from tying her shoelaces to using oven mitts. It was like becoming a child all over again. They wouldn't let her leave the hospital until she could prove she could safely make a cup of tea for her mother, who nursed her daily.

Hard does not mean impossible.

Waking up each day, Kris often felt a deep anger at the universe for saving her from the accident. She grappled with severe fatigue and rage, popping painkillers and antibiotics like candy for years. Her recovery was not a sprint but an ultramarathon – a slow, laborious and demanding journey that stretched on endlessly. Kris's path was filled with relentless challenges, but it was also a testament to her unyielding spirit, her brave mindset and the fierce, messy process of healing.

Over time Kris came to see the accident not as something that happened to her, but *for* her.

Before the accident, she had been aimlessly wandering through life working in a pub, pouring beers.

After the accident, Kris had been told she would never earn more than a minimum wage, due to her impaired learning ability. She decided she wanted to prove everyone wrong. She found purpose, direction and momentum. She had always wanted to work in IT, so relentlessly applied for jobs, eventually becoming a top performer in her first role. She consistently tapped into a deep, endless well of grit within her – the strength of her brave mindset.

Years later, she found herself in the grips of yet another health crisis, enduring daily battles with diarrhoea and relentless nausea. The diagnosis? Fructose malabsorption and leaky gut. This marked the beginning of a profound journey into the world of gut health. She recalls, 'Discovering bone broth was like finding a magic elixir.'

For the next two years, she threw herself wholeheartedly into learning everything about gut health, determined to reclaim her health and well-being with the same fierce tenacity that had carried her through so many other challenges.

Recovering from her accident and healing her gut health became a series of *Little Brave Acts* that spanned over 15 years. Thus, the accident was a catalyst for her enduring personal development journey. Without it, she wouldn't have gained her vast knowledge and wisdom about gut health and overall well-being. Kris needed immense resilience and courage to get through those years, but deep down she knew this was the meaning for which she had been searching. The universe had a plan, and she embraced it, one brave act at a time.

As Kris and I worked together, she also learned about the importance of expanding her vision to help more women. We delved deeper into healing unsurfaced childhood traumas, and I showed her how to manage her emotions and to process uncomfortable memories from her past. Kris started writing her own book and speaking about her personal story of resilience. I had immense respect for her commitment to the work.

So, remember this: when life throws you off your bike and over the top of a car, it might just be the beginning of your greatest transformation. Keep pushing, keep believing and keep doing those little steps – the hallmark of the brave mindset.

Because sometimes, what feels like the end is just the start of something extraordinary.

Alicia's powerful little step: finding resilience

'I've said Parkinson's is a gift. It's the gift that keeps on taking, but it has changed my life in so many positive ways.'

– MICHAEL J. FOX

I know so commonly when we face a crisis, when we're stripped raw and left vulnerable, that's when we truly start to listen to our inner selves. It's in these moments of profound suffering that the whispers of our soul, usually drowned out by the clamour of everyday life, become clear. It's here, in the depths of our pain, that we uncover our spiritual gifts – the deep wells of intuition, empathy and resilience that have always been within us, waiting to be discovered.

Alicia came to work with me, driven by a longing for spiritual and intuitive knowledge. I sensed there was a deeper story, and in our very first session, she shared the experience that cracked her wide open.

'My second pregnancy was so much easier. No migraines, no illness – it was such a relief. At our routine 32-week check-up, I saw Isabella's heart beating strong, and everything looked good. I was excited; it was our wedding anniversary that weekend, and we were going out to celebrate.

'After the weekend, though, my instinct told me something was not right, even though my head kept convincing me everything was okay. I called the doctor and was asked to come in for an ultrasound.'

254

As I listened to Alicia, a stone sank into the pit of my stomach.

'I was lying there with the cold ultrasound machine against my belly. There was a heaviness in the air and time slowed down. Then I heard the words that no pregnant woman ever wants to hear, "I am so sorry, there is no heartbeat."'

There are moments in life that shatter us, breaking us into pieces so small we wonder if we'll ever be whole again. Stillbirth is one of those moments. It's the silent, brutal thief that robs us of our dreams, our hopes and our future in an instant. It's a pain so profound it can leave us gasping for breath, wondering how we'll ever find the strength to stand again.

Isabella passed away at 33 weeks. Alicia was about to enter the darkest period of her life. One that asked for a grit and resilience many never face in a lifetime.

'I called my husband. I was in shock and disbelief. It was the hardest phone call I had ever had to make. We went to the hospital to deliver her that night.'

What happens when the natural order of birth and death is reversed? When you walk into a birthing suite expecting to meet midwives and doctors, but instead you find yourself speaking with funeral homes and social workers? This was Alicia's stark and heartbreaking reality.

Alicia's grief was colossal, swallowing her whole. Experiencing stillbirth is like being thrown into the deepest, darkest ocean, forced to find your way back to the surface one agonising stroke at a time.

In the weeks and months that followed, Alicia would spend time reading other women's and families' stories online. She was not searching for the 'how' – the doctors had already answered that question for her. She was searching for the 'why', and she realised this was the question other women were searching for too. It's a question with no answer, a silent scream into the void.

Eight years later she is now a fierce advocate, determined to help prevent others from experiencing this heartache. On reflection, I also realised how deeply uncomfortable her situation had made me feel at the time. I wanted a resolution for Alicia, a complete healing that would ease my own discomfort. Now eight years later, I wanted the reassurance that the 'why' had led to her greater purpose. But she never found the why. What she found was her own resilience and capacity for grief and survival.

She said, 'I am the same Alicia, but also different. I am more than I was or thought I could be.' Alicia was describing grit. She reflected, 'Life will forever be a combination of joy and grief and I am at peace with that.'

This is the kind of brave mindset that many of us are called to understand – to find peace in not knowing the 'why', and to walk forward holding both joy and grief. It's about embracing the messy, beautiful paradox of life and learning to thrive within it.

This extends far beyond the horror of stillbirth.

We may not have had the childhood we wanted and need to process the grief as adults. We may have a marriage dissolve suddenly, a loss that feels like a death. In such dark times, we learn the true meaning of resilience: as adults we must learn to live our lives holding both joy and grief simultaneously. Understanding that this is possible, and even required of us, is crucial. It helps silence the persistent voice in our head that constantly asks, 'Why?'

Why did he leave?

Why was I beaten as a child?

Why did they have to die?

Emotional grit asks us to go beyond such questions and find a way to live with the duality and conflicting emotions that life throws at us. We discover that we can endure far more than we ever thought possible. We come to understand that our hearts, though broken, are incredibly powerful and capable of infinite love and compassion.

Alicia reflected on the profound lessons she had learned about self-care and giving herself the grace and time to heal, understanding that healing is not a straight path – there will be good and bad days. She learned to be gentle with herself, to nurture her wounded heart with the same care and compassion we'd offer a dear friend. She learned about the fragility of life and that every moment is a blessing.

On challenging days, 'I bring my other children close to me and hold them tight, smothering them with kisses.'

Alicia learned to live more fully and presently, embracing each moment with the fierce love and gratitude that comes from knowing just how precious life truly is.

These are the gifts we all seek – to live a full and present life. We may not realise that the human experience teaches us this primarily through loss. We will all have to endure loss – the loss of our parents, which is the natural order of life, or the loss of a partner, sibling or a good friend. At some point, we too will all need to learn how to walk forward holding joy and grief simultaneously. This is the essence of being human: to embrace this beautiful, messy duality of life.

Finding a guide

'One of the greatest values of mentors is the ability to see ahead what others cannot see and to help them navigate a course to their destination.'

– JOHN C. MAXWELL

When venturing towards Plan C and navigating the failures of our previous plans, you need a cheer squad, a mentor, a soul mother, a visionary woman (or man) who can help you see a future that's in your blind spot. These incredible people, who have mastered resilience through their own *Little Brave Acts*, will be your guides. They are the rule-breakers, the ones who know how to rise after falling. They will hold your hand and gently nudge you forward. When things get tough, they will help you stay the course, reminding you of your strength, your vision and your worth. You don't have to do this alone; let these wise souls light your way.

For me, that guiding light was my IVF doctor, Dr Raewyn Teirney.

'Fuck, fuck, fuck,' she declared, surprising the camera crew with her expletives. Dr Raewyn was also being filmed by the *Big Miracles* television crew. There she was, in a designer floral pink dress, with multiple degrees framed behind her on the office wall, dropping F-bombs like a sailor. Everyone was shocked by her outburst.

She was actually expressing the profound relief of just having given us the positive news that I was pregnant. She, too, was relieved after delivering countless phone calls with bad news. It was a raw, unfiltered moment that captured the emotional rollercoaster of our journey.

I couldn't have asked for a better cheerleader and soul mother on my path. Navigating the insane world of IVF, you need someone who can curse like a trucker and then hug you like a mum. This was Dr Raewyn for me.

When we are navigating the challenges of embracing our Plan C, we need to lean into the sage wisdom and experiences of those who have lived through similar trials. We must seek them out and rely on their support. We need the empathy of those who have traversed the tough roads before us. This path is rarely one we can walk alone, and if we try, we will find ourselves hitting roadblocks that feel insurmountable without help.

I met Dr Raewyn at a YouTube workshop five years ago, back before Instagram Reels and TikTok were even a thing. We bonded over whispered conversations and mutual confusion, struggling with the long, technical process of creating videos manually.

She was launching her conception app and fertility video course, and I was stepping into my role as a business mentor. In one of those hushed exchanges, I shared my desperation to become a mother. Dr Raewyn, with her characteristic candour, shared her own fertility story: 'You know, I only realised I wanted to be a mother at 37. I had finished studying obstetrics and gynaecology and was just completing my fertility studies. The irony was that my fertility window was closing right at that point. I met my husband at 43, and he had prostate cancer, so he couldn't produce sperm. The IVF techniques we have now weren't available back then, so I had no choice but to give up on my dream.'

Her story struck a chord with me. Here was a woman who had dedicated her life to helping others conceive, only to face her own fertility challenges just as she discovered her desire for motherhood. It was a reminder that even those who seem to have it all figured out face their own struggles and uncertainties.

Five years later, when I met Tyson, I immediately called Dr Raewyn.

Dr Raewyn became not just a doctor, but a mentor and a friend, someone who understood the journey intimately and could offer both professional and personal wisdom.

We need the Little Brave Act *of seeking guides and mentors on our journey.*

As we navigated each round of IVF, Dr Raewyn was there, understanding the pang of pain if I didn't become a mother. She knew the fear of being childless. One day, after an appointment, I asked her if her experience made her a better IVF doctor. She responded, her eyes glazed with tears, 'Definitely. I have empathy. When patients bring their babies, I love it, but it creates a pang in my heart. It never leaves. I see women who desperately want to be mothers, and I hear their fears. They're scared their partner will leave them or that they won't have a fulfilling life. They believe something is wrong with them.'

From her lived experience, Dr Raewyn had a well of empathy and wisdom to draw from. 'I help women stay determined, to not give up, and to keep trying different approaches. I want to see them succeed.'

During the two years I traversed the fertility path, Dr Raewyn provided the knowledge I needed, the empathy as I cried in her office, and the nudge forward when it was time to pivot and start the donor egg process. Her disappointment at finding herself childless became a motivation for her to help so many women. Upon reflection, I drew on her determination for myself.

Our guides will be invested in our journey – in our Plan C.

In addition to my IVF journey, I've sought guides in many aspects of my life, and you will too. We need spiritual teachers to remind us of our deepest truths and mentors to push us beyond our comfort zones. We need guides to show us the way when we're lost and healers to mend our broken hearts. Counsellors help us understand our childhoods, while shamans help us birth new versions of ourselves. And let's not forget the wise older women who have walked this road before us – they are living libraries, rich with stories and wisdom.

We hesitate to reach out to mentors and guides because we've been taught to value independence above all else, to believe that needing help is a sign of weakness. We're afraid of being vulnerable, of admitting we don't have it all figured out. There's this voice in our heads that says, 'You should be able to do this on your own.' But the truth is, asking for help is one of the bravest things we can do. It's a little step to say, 'I need guidance. I need some help. I am feeling lost.' It's how we grow, how we heal, how we become the women we're meant to be.

Dr Raewyn went on to become one of the leading fertility experts in her field. While she was a Doctor of Science, she was also a Doctor of the Heart. She showed me that embracing Plan C isn't about settling − it's about finding a new path that leads to unexpected and successful destinations. These paths were not available to her over 30 years ago and she wished that they were.

Brave truths

- When you master your mind through a brave mindset, you will master your life.

- True strength is found in the moments when you decide to try again through *Little Brave Acts*, despite the setbacks.

- Dreams never die: they just become unlived. It's never too late to breathe life back into them and make them a reality.

- Succeed not despite of who you are. Succeed because of who you are. Tough things happen to all of us. It's how we rise from them that defines our strength.

- You will need a guide who has taken *Little Brave Acts* themselves who can show you the way.

Brave questions

- How can you reframe your current obstacles as opportunities for growth and learning? In what ways can you celebrate your progress and acknowledge your efforts, no matter how small they may seem?

- What little step can you take today to move closer to your goals, even when the going gets tough?

- What is your 'why' - the deeper purpose or motivation that drives you to stay the course?

- How can you practise self-compassion and patience with yourself during difficult times?

- What *Little Brave Acts* can you take to find a mentor, guide or coach to support you on your path?

Brave mantra

I am stronger than I know and braver than I believe.

CHAPTER 14

Big miracles

'When Plan B fails, and C and D and so on, it's just life reminding you to trust in your own power to keep creating new paths. The alphabet is infinite when it comes to your strength.'

– GLENNON DOYLE

I don't believe that miracles are rare. And I don't believe that miracles are always big, grand, earth-shaking events. My life has taught me that miracles are often small and common. They are the tiny moments of grace that whisper to us when we least expect it. Yet these small miracles that we experience privately do evoke *big* feelings, reminding us that magic is woven into the fabric of our everyday lives.

After appearing on the television show *Big Miracles,* so many people shared with me their miracle baby story. And thus confirmed my belief that miracles were as common and as special as sunrises and sunsets. They happen daily and if we stop and acknowledge them, we can experience awe daily too. But most of us are too busy to ask for a miracle or even notice that the universe is bestowing them on us.

When you believe in miracles, you will see them everywhere.

Miracles are the laughter that bubbles up from deep within you when you thought you'd forgotten how to laugh. It's in the kindness of a stranger who sees your struggle and offers a hand. It's in the quiet resolve to keep going, to keep trying, to keep believing that better days are ahead. It's that moment when you look in the mirror and, for the first time in forever, you see yourself not through the lens of your failures or fears, but through the eyes of your resilience and strength.

A miracle is when you've been through the storm – divorce, heartbreak, loss – and you've felt every gut-wrenching wave crash over you, but somehow, you've found a way to keep swimming. It's the silent strength of a single mum tucking her kids into bed after a long day, knowing she's doing the best she can with what she has. It's the courage to dream again, even when the world tells you to be realistic.

My big miracles

'Things work out best for those who make the best of how things work out. Plan your path, but be open to miracles along the way.'

– JOHN WOODEN

There are two cameras trailing us, capturing every step as the obstetricians and anaesthetist lead us into the delivery ward. Yes, we are being filmed again. Our two-and-a-half-year journey of trying for a child is finally coming to an end, and I am minutes away from delivery. The next chapter of our life is about to begin.

As I'm being wheeled into the operating theatre, my heart races and my breath comes short and quick. I glance at my husband and see a whirlwind of emotions behind his eyes – anxiety, excitement and a host of feelings he's never experienced before. He squeezes my hand, grounding us both in this unforgettable moment.

A blue sheet goes up in front of my face, shielding me from the intense intrusion of a C-section. Despite the room being filled with ten people, it becomes silent – a heavy, anticipatory silence. I can hear the obstetrician giving gentle, calm instructions to the nurses around her. The only interruption is the steady bleeping of the heart monitor.

Time feels suspended for what seems like an eternity but is only ten seconds. Then, just like in the movies, I hear the high-pitched scream of my son. He is born at 36 weeks, considered an early pre-term. They whisk him away to a side bench to check his vital signs. My husband Tyson, tears streaming down his face, cuts the umbilical cord. And then, in a moment of pure magic, our son is plonked onto my chest. The weight of him, the warmth of him, it's all so surreal and overwhelming. The journey, the struggle, it all fades away as I hold my miracle in my arms.

I hold him, wailing, 'I can't believe he is mine. I can't believe he is mine.' It's a mantra of disbelief and overwhelming joy. I had given up hope many times, but never the dream. There were moments when the grit required felt unbearable. I grappled with the uncertainty of choosing to carry a child not biologically connected to me, yet I held the vision clear and strong in my head and heart.

On 11 April, a miracle entered our lives. We named him Phoenix – a symbol of resurrection and triumph over adversity. He is the embodiment of our journey, our struggles, and our unwavering belief in the power of love and vision. Phoenix, our little miracle, was here, and he is ours.

Let's hit the pause button on this story.

I get it – the life of a child is often described as a miracle. And I know not everyone gets a baby at the end of IVF, or even through a donor or surrogacy process. But here's what I know for sure: if we hadn't conceived Phoenix, we would have found another way to nurture, love, and parent. Just a week before the donor implant procedure, I turned to Tyson and asked flatly, 'What if this doesn't work? What if it's just us? Will I be enough? Will this be enough – our marriage?'

He pulled me close, looked me straight in the eyes and gave me a passionate kiss. Then we sat down and talked about another life, a different one. In my heart, I knew that even if this path didn't lead us to a baby, *Little Brave Acts* would carry us through the heartache and beyond. We would have found another big miracle. Because love isn't about the exact picture you've painted in your head. Love is about the willingness to show up, to adapt, to keep moving forward even when the path radically changes.

The journey to your Plan C will stretch you and
test you in ways you never knew possible.

The big miracle was *who* I became in this process. I didn't birth my son, my son birthed me. I transformed into the woman I had dreamed of being many years ago. The journey of taking little steps allowed me to connect passionately with my purpose – coaching women and becoming a motivational speaker – especially around fertility struggles.

I became a woman who could safely open her heart and love generously. I healed the relationships with my parents – relationships that had been strained for so many years. There was a time when this felt out of reach, impossible even. But through the work, through the tears and the struggle, I found my way back to them, and to myself.

I became a woman who slowed down, smiled more and laughed loudly. The too-serious, tightly coiled version of me unwound through countless moments of healing and doing the inner work.

I let go of the need to control everything, embraced the chaos and found joy in the unpredictability of life.

I finally embodied the qualities I needed to be the mother I wanted to be. In that moment, the universe whispered, 'Yes, you are ready. I will make you a mother.' And that was the true miracle. The universe saw that I had become the woman I was meant to be, and she said, 'Now, you are ready for this next chapter.'

Illusion of control

Even when we step into our unexpected and unconventional Plan Cs and beyond, don't be surprised if the illusion of control – that *we* are in control – still lingers. That control gives us the safety and certainty we all crave and perhaps always will. Here's the thing: I've learned that life is a dance between control and surrender. We clutch onto control because it feels safe, it feels like we have a handle on things. But the truth is, real growth, real magic, happens in the surrender. It's in letting go, trusting the process, and embracing the uncertainty that we find our true strength and resilience.

Michael Singer, in *The Surrender Experiment*, shares a similar journey of unexpected paths. He writes, 'The natural unfolding of the universe takes care of everything. I learned to let go of my personal preferences and trust the flow of life.' Singer's experience highlights that surrendering to the unexpected can lead to profound growth and fulfilment, even when the path is not what we initially envisioned. When we do, we open ourselves to the miracles waiting to unfold. The more little steps we take in life, the easier and more masterful we become at surrendering.

The number one worry for many donor egg recipients is, 'Will I bond with my baby?' This fear haunted me from the moment I embarked on my journey to become a donor mum. So, I did everything I could to mitigate it. I chose donor eggs from a woman with dark chocolate coloured skin, just like mine. I prayed for a little dark-skinned daughter who would be a reflection of me. I believed that if she looked into her mother's brown eyes and brown skin, matching her own, she would see herself. I thought this would ease my worry. I thought this would make us love each other more, where biology was absent.

But life, in all her wisdom, had a lesson for me about surrender and the truth that love transcends skin colour. When my son Phoenix arrived with pale Irish skin, blonde hair and blue eyes, like Tyson, I laughed out loud. The love and bond we shared was instant, immediate and immense. In that moment, I realised the depth of my capacity to love. Over the following months, his blue eyes would look into my brown eyes, and we shared a knowing bond. We had finally found our way into each other's lives, proving that love knows no bounds and that true connection goes far beyond physical appearance. Phoenix showed me that love doesn't need matching sets. Love is wild and free and shows up in the most unexpected packages. It turns out, the miracle wasn't in our matching looks but in the boundless love we discovered together.

Discovering our purpose

The pursuit of Plan C and beyond is where we often find our true purpose and deeper meaning in life. When the plans we meticulously crafted fall apart, new paths open up in the most unexpected ways. It's in those detours and unplanned journeys that we uncover who we really are and what we're meant to do. When Plan A and B crumble, Plan C emerges from the rubble, guiding us towards a life richer and more fulfilling than we ever imagined.

IVF and fertility challenges *are* still taboo, though I only realised this after hundreds and hundreds of women (and men) reached out to me, sharing their 'that is us too' stories.

These stories told me that IVF is not just about making babies, but birthing mothers – mothers of courage, mothers of audacity, mothers who refuse to be defined by what their bodies can or cannot do.

I recently spoke on a panel at the Donor Egg and Surrogacy Conference in Sydney, a place I never expected to be. My career as a motivational speaker had taken an interesting turn, and now I was sharing my story with rooms full of women and men seeking guidance, insights and the kind of raw, real stories that speak to the heart of navigating a fertility journey with *Little Brave Acts*. I thought I had found my purpose, so I stopped looking. But then, a deeper level within my purpose found its way to me. Life is not about finding one grand purpose, but about embracing the many purposes that find you along the way. Our purpose evolves with us and quite often each one shapes us and leads us to the next.

We often have more than one purpose in life.

There I was, addressing these incredible women and men, realising that our greatest missions often find us, not through the plans we make, but through the ones that fall apart. It was in this unexpected space, on this unplanned path, in the pursuit of Plan C, that I realised our greatest missions often come to us not through our plans, but through the paths we never planned to take.

Plan D, E, F, G and beyond ...

Months after the arrival of Phoenix, I am covered in breast milk, Tyson is singing lullabies and there are new smile and fatigue lines etched on both of our faces. We are deep in the beautiful, chaotic haze of having a newborn. Amidst the sleepless nights and endless nappy changes, we find ourselves talking about giving Phoenix a sibling. We still have three frozen donor embryos, and the idea of expanding our family fills our hearts with hope and excitement.

We're also dreaming about buying a family home, travelling and working in the USA. Plan D, E, and F are unfolding before us, but we no longer see them as mere plans. This journey together has taught us the power of surrender, of letting go of our rigid expectations and embracing a life that could be beyond our wildest dreams. We've learned that when we trust the process and each other, the universe has a way of guiding us to places more magical than we ever imagined.

Our lives are no longer about meticulous plans and control; they're about love, faith and surrender. Every step we take is a dance with the universe. And in this dance, I will continue to take *Little Brave Acts* to make our dreams happen. Because these small steps into the unknown with an open heart have carried us this far and will carry us further still. So here we are, in the midst of this messy, unpredictable, glorious life, knowing that whatever comes next, we'll face it together, with open hearts, open hands and endless bravery.

Brave truths

- **When you believe in miracles you will start to see miracles in every part of your life.**
- **We have more than one purpose in life, and surrendering to the unfolding path will lead us to our many different purposes.**
- **We will constantly dance between the need to control our life and the need to surrender.**
- **The journey to your Plan C will stretch you and test you in ways you never knew possible, so don't resist the transformation.**
- **An authentic life is lived by taking *Little Brave Acts* daily and inspiring others to do so as well.**

Brave questions

- What aspects of your life have you been trying to control, and how have they hindered your growth and happiness?

- In what ways can you invite miracles into your life by being open to unexpected opportunities and trusting the flow of the universe?

- What *Little Brave Acts* can you take today to surrender your need for control and allow life to unfold naturally?

- How can you shift your perspective to see Plan C as a divine intervention, guiding you towards your true purpose and ultimate happiness?

- How can you make small, brave steps a part of your daily, weekly and monthly routine? And how can you inspire others in your life to take *Little Brave Acts*.

Brave mantra

I create big miracles in my life through *Little Brave Acts*.

Acknowledgments

As I reach the final pages of this book, I am filled with immense gratitude for the many hands, hearts and minds that have contributed to its creation. Writing is often seen as a solitary endeavour, but this journey has been anything but lonely. It has been enriched by the support, encouragement and wisdom of so many. To those who have walked alongside me, offering guidance, inspiration and unwavering belief in this work, I owe a debt of thanks that words can hardly express.

To the brave women who generously shared their stories for this book: Caroline Clarke, Emma MacCarthy, Leah Scott, Erica Kelly, Morgan Willoughby, Lynne Deshler, Heather Debra, Kris Picker, Alicia Mitchell, Alice Cheng, Ange Teulon, Eleanor Mills, Dr Raewyn Teirney and Jan Herdman – thank you. Your voices and experiences have brought this book to life, and I am profoundly grateful for your contributions.

To Sinead Brace, my right hand, who is always one step ahead – thank you for being an indispensable part of my business journey.

Just as it takes a village to raise a child, it takes an incredible team to bring a book to life. I am deeply grateful to the amazing team at Rockpool Publishing for their unwavering support and expertise. A heartfelt thank you to Lisa Hanrahan and Paul Dennett for your visionary leadership, to Katie Stackhouse for your patience and guidance, and to Sara Lindberg for the cover design. To the entire team, your hard work and dedication have made this journey possible, and I am truly thankful.

My deepest thanks to Laurel Cohn for being an invaluable sounding board and an exceptional guide throughout the writing process. Your insights and editorial expertise have been instrumental. I also want to extend my gratitude to Zena Shapter and Gabiann Marin for their unwavering support in helping shape the roadmap of this book.

To my spiritual mentors and guides thank you for shining the light when I have found myself in the dark: Louise Winchester, Michelle Masters, Tom Cronin, Ricky Abbonizio and Avril Norman.

In a world that's always shifting and pulling us in a million directions, there's something sacred about those girlfriends who've been by your side forever. They are the ones who've seen every version of you – every messy, beautiful, and evolving piece of your life – and they still love you fiercely. Thank you Darlean Williams, Alex Thompson, Kath Haling and Toni Borthwick.

To my soul friends – we found each other in this lifetime: Tammi Kirkness, Anne Miles, Tatjana Genys, Jessica Lee, Janet Testaz, Nina Concepcion, Ali Daddo, Dominique Hutchison, Lali Wiratunga, Lisa Martin, Kyane Vives, Andrew Flannery, Caroline Lepron, Charmain Melosi, Antonia Geracec, Chloe Brault, Nicky Pullen, Helen Garner, Sabia Vardy, Michelle Sutherland, Tarryn Ellison, Tricha Tippapart, Tiffany Scott, Pip Drysdale, Andres Engracia, Shaunagh Keenan.

Thank you to the doctors, nurses and scientists at IVF Australia, in particular Dr Raewyn Teirney for your humanity and soul. The incredible team at Ronde Media for your vision and mission: Liam Taylor, Chris Merran, Antonia Osili, Sammy Sheldon, Kathryn Milliss. Thank you, Dr Kath Whitton, for delivering our precious cargo.

To my mother, father and sisters. I am who I am because of you, and I carry your lessons and love with me in everything I do. To Tyson's family – thank you for embracing me with open arms and making me feel like one of your own.

To my beloved Tyson – I have loved you across a million lifetimes. Thank you for finding me in this one and joining me on this wild ride. Your unwavering support has helped me create the mental, physical and spiritual space I needed to bring this book to life. I am endlessly grateful to have you by my side.

To all the lightworkers, authors, soul mentors, visionaries, thought leaders, psychologists, yogis and spiritual teachers who came before me – I see you. I stand on your broad, brave shoulders, and because of you, I've learned to see that same light, wisdom and courage within myself. You've guided me home to who I really am, and for that, I am forever grateful. Thank you.

Bibliography

Bridges, William. *The Way of Transition: Embracing Life's Most Difficult Moments*, DaCapo Press, 2001.

Bridges, William. *Transitions: Making Sense of Life's Changes*, Da Capo Press, revised edition 2004 (originally published 1980).

Brown, Brené. *Braving the Wilderness*, Random House, 2017.

Chödrön, Pema. *When Things Fall Apart: Heart Advice for Difficult Times*, Shambhala, 2016 (20th Anniversary edition).

Clance, P. R. & Imes, S. A. 'The imposter phenomenon in high achieving women: Dynamics and therapeutic intervention', *Psychotherapy: Theory, Research & Practice*, 15(3), 241–247, 1978, doi.org/10.1037/h0086006.

de Berker, A., Rutledge, R., Mathys, C. et al. 'Computations of uncertainty mediate acute stress responses in humans', *Nature Communications*, 7, 10996, 2016, doi.org/10.1038/ncomms10996

DeMartini, John. *Inspired Relationships*, DeMartini Institute, [n.d.] drdemartini.com/multimedia_content/bte_special/inspired_relationships_ebook.pdf

Doyle, Glennon. *Untamed: Stop Pleasing, Start Living*, Vermilion, 2020.

Feiler, Bruce. *Life is in the Transitions: Mastering Change at Any Age*, Penguin Press, 2020.

Gay, Roxane. *Hunger: A Memoir of (My) Body*, HarperCollins, 2017.

Hawkins, David. *Power vs. Force: The Hidden Determinants of Human Behavior*, Hay House, 2013.

Hendricks, Gay. *The Big Leap: Conquer Your Hidden Fear and Take Life to the Next Level*, HarperCollins, 2010.

Holiday, Ryan. *Obstacle is the Way: The Ancient Art of Turning Adversity to Advantage*, Profile Books, 2014.

Hyatt, Michael. *The Vision Driven Leader: 10 Questions to Focus Your Efforts, Energize Your Team, and Scale Your Business*, Baker Books, 2020.

Kaiser, Shannon. *The Self-Love Experiment: Fifteen Principles for Becoming More Kind, Compassionate, and Accepting of Yourself*, Tarcher, 2017.

Karlgaard, Rich. *Late Bloomers: The Power of Patience in a World Obsessed with Early Achievement*, Crown, 2019.

'Maggie Kuhn', en.wikipedia.org/wiki/Maggie_Kuhn.

Maxwell, John C. *Failing Forward: Turning Mistakes into Stepping Stones for Success*, HarperCollins, 2016.

McArdle, Megan. *The Up Side of Down: Why Failing Well Is the Key to Success*, Penguin Books, 2014.

Mills, Eleanor. *Much More to Come: Lessons on the Mahem and Magnificence of Midlife*, HarperCollins, 2024.

Singer, Michael. *The Surrender Experiment: My Journey Into Life's Perfection*, Harmony, 2015.

Young, Valerie. *The Secret Thoughts of Successful Women: Why Capable People Suffer from the Impostor Syndrome and How to Thrive in Spite of It*, Crown, 2011.

Staying connected with Sheila

Say hello:

Website: sheilav.co
Instagram: @sheila_v__
LinkedIn: Sheila Vijeyarasa
Sheila loves hearing about the brave transformations in your life. Share your *Little Brave Act* by emailing her at info@sheilav.co

Gifts for you:

Receive a copy of The Brave Woman toolkit today by going to sheilav.co/free-gifts

Podcast:

Listen to *Brave Conversations* on Apple Podcasts, Spotify and YouTube.

Courses:

Check out The Brave Woman program at sheilav.co

Motivational speaking and training:

Book Sheila Vijeyarasa as your next conference speaker at sheilav.co/speaker, or collaborate with her to inspire your leaders through her signature Brave Leader program.

About the author

Author, keynote speaker, business mentor, corporate coach and spiritual medium

From corporate C-suite CFO to empowerment mentor, Sheila Vijeyarasa is a force of transformation. Following the successful release of her debut book, *Brave: Courageously Live Your Truth*, Sheila continues to inspire with her unique blend of corporate expertise and spiritual wisdom.

Sheila's mission is clear: bringing spirituality into the business world isn't about new age trends – it's about fostering courageous and conscious leadership in today's complex and consequential corporate landscape. With an MBA and over 20 years' experience in senior roles across accounting, banking, media and publishing, Sheila experienced a profound awakening during her corporate journey. This awakening led her to cultivate her mediumship skills in England, master emergent mindfulness in the US, and immerse herself in the transcendental teachings of the ancient Vedas in India.

Driven by a desire to help others discover their true purpose and build fulfilling lives, Sheila has seamlessly merged her corporate acumen with her intuitive wisdom. Her international bestseller, *Brave: Courageously Live Your Truth*, has been hailed as a 'comprehensive spiritual guidebook' for conscious corporate leaders, solidifying her reputation as a sought-after motivational speaker.

As the founder of The Brave Woman™ mentoring program, Sheila has become a beacon of light and support for women worldwide. She also bravely shares her personal journey to motherhood, including her mature-age IVF experience, on an Australian television documentary *Big Miracles*.

Sheila is a powerful manifester and a spiritual teacher, mentor, intuitive guide and executive coach who has already supported hundreds of women on their path to authentic living. She empowers her clients to adopt a holistic, spiritual approach to both their careers and personal lives, helping emerging leaders clear limiting beliefs and overcome blocks like burnout, perfectionism and imposter syndrome.

With decades of leadership experience, Sheila possesses an extensive toolkit of high-performance habits, confidence hacks and communication strategies for navigating challenging staff and difficult conversations. As a keynote speaker, Sheila delivers powerful truths that compel her audiences to honour themselves and connect with their own intuition and inner truth.

Sheila's insights and strategies for leading an empowering and courageous life have been featured in media outlets such as Thrive Global, *The Sydney Morning Herald*, *Body + Soul*, *CEO World Magazine*, and *CFO Australia*, among others.

Also by Sheila Vijeyarasa

Brave
Courageously live your truth
ISBN: 9781925946406

Brave: Courageously live your truth sets out a clear roadmap for women to reclaim their personal power, providing them with the knowledge and courage to step into an authentic life.

This book helps to identify your personal calling, recognising a destiny that yearns to be fulfilled and provides the skills to recognise the power and courage within to take the leap towards a more meaningful and passionate life.

This book is for the woman who feels lost in the midst of all the small decisions in her life. Be it following a career path, climbing the corporate ladder or caring for family, sometimes your focus, personal beliefs and goals get lost in the day to day. Now is the time to identify your personal calling and rediscover the destiny that is meant for you alone.

Discover how to regain connection to the feminine, emotional and intuitive core of one's being. *Brave: Courageously live your truth* provides the tools to make the changes to be true to yourself and follow your dreams. It shows you the answers that lie within and encourages you to embrace your individuality and that life should not be a 'one size fits all' approach.

This is a step-by-step guide to assist with making the changes to be able to courageously live an authentic life. Including case studies and helpful insights along the way, readers can tailor the lessons to suit their individual work/life circumstances. This is the ultimate handbook to develop the lifelong skills to embrace the power within, accept your vulnerability to develop resilience and strength to tackle whatever challenges that life sends your way.